TWIST

Miles Tredinnick's first stage play *Because of Mr Darrow* was performed at the Finborough Arms Theatre in London in 1983. This was followed by *Laugh? I Nearly Went to Miami!* which premiered at the Pentameters Theatre in Hampstead before appearing as part of the first Liverpool Festival of Comedy. His other stage plays include *Up Pompeii*, *It's Now or Never!* and the four one-act *Topless* plays set on open-top sightseeing buses in London, Philadelphia, Sydney, and Las Vegas. For television Miles has created and written the BBC1 series *Wyatt's Watchdogs*, and co-wrote the Frankie Howerd TV special *Superfrank*. He was a writer on *Birds of a Feather* and has written a novel, *Fripp*. In addition to his writing, under the stage name of Riff Regan, Miles is the lead singer of the English punk band *London*.

TWIST

by Miles Tredinnick

JOSEF WEINBERGER PLAYS

LONDON

TWIST
First published in 2018
by Josef Weinberger Ltd
12-14 Mortimer Street, London W1T 3JJ
www.josef-weinberger.com / plays@jwmail.co.uk

Copyright © 2018 by Miles Tredinnick
Copyright © 1990 by Miles Tredinnick as an unpublished dramatic composition

The author asserts his moral right to be identified as the author of the work.

ISBN: 978 0 85676 375 5

This play is protected by Copyright. According to Copyright Law, no public performance or reading of a protected play or part of that play may be given without prior authorization from Josef Weinberger Plays, as agent for the Copyright Owners.

From time to time it is necessary to restrict or even withdraw the rights of certain plays. It is therefore essential to check with us before making a commitment to produce a play.

NO PERFORMANCE MAY BE GIVEN WITHOUT A LICENCE

AMATEUR PRODUCTIONS
Royalties are due at least one calendar month prior to the first performance. A royalty quotation will be issued upon receipt of the following details:

Name of Licensee
Play Title
Place of Performance
Dates and Number of Performances
Audience Capacity and ticket price(s)

PROFESSIONAL PRODUCTIONS
All enquiries regarding professional rights should be addressed to the author, c/o Josef Weinberger Plays at the address above.

OVERSEAS PRODUCTIONS
Applications for productions overseas should be made to our local authorised agents. Further information can be found on our website or in our printed Catalogue of Plays.

CONDITIONS OF SALE
This book is sold subject to the condition that it shall not by way of trade or otherwise be re-sold, hired out, circulated or distributed without prior consent of the Publisher. **Reproduction of the text either in whole or part and by any means is strictly forbidden.**

This book has been typeset in sans-serif fonts to assist with accessibility for visually impaired readers.

Printed by Edward Dudfield Ltd.

TWIST (under the title *Getting Away with Murder*) was first presented by Priory Productions at the Pentameters Theatre, London on February 14th 1995 with the following cast:

> DAVID WOODS................ Simon Kane
>
> SARAH SEETON................ Sandra Hale
>
> MRS BECK .... Rosemary Smith
>
> ROBERT WOODS.............. Robert Wilby
>
> HANNAH VAN LEE .... Jude Jacubowski
>
> INSPECTOR ROOT............ Sid Dhant
>
> Designed by Martin Gallagher
> Lighting Design by Alan Colclough
> Technical Advisor: Graeme Curry
> Directed by Stephen Warden

In 2018 the premiere UK tour of **TWIST** was produced by Baroque Theatre Company with the following cast:

> DAVID WOODS................ Clive Greenwood
>
> SARAH SEETON................ Thea Balich
>
> MRS BECK .... Claire Bibby
>
> ROBERT WOODS.............. Ellis J. Wells
>
> HANNAH VAN LEE .... Claire Bibby
>
> INSPECTOR ROOT............ Ellis J. Wells
>
> Set Design and Build: Matt Nunn
> Costume Designer: Suzanne Bell
> Stage Manager: Samson Robinson
> Lighting and Sound Technician: Simon Moss
> Produced by Claire Bibby
> Directed by Adam Morley

CHARACTERS

David Woods
Sarah Seeton
Mrs Beck
Robert Woods
Hannah Van Lee
Inspector Root

SETTING

The action takes place in a flat in South Kensington, London, the home of David Woods, and his wife Sarah Seeton.

Time: The present

SCENES

ACT ONE
Scene One .... A morning in February
Scene Two .... Fifteen minutes later
Scene Three ...... That afternoon
Scene Four .... Fifty minutes later

ACT TWO
Scene One .... The same – the action is continuous
Scene Two .... Late afternoon, nine months later

ACT ONE

Scene One

The action of the play takes place in David Woods *and* Sarah Seeton's *South Kensington flat in London. It is situated on the first floor of a mansion block that houses seven other similar apartments. It's a composite set of lounge R, and kitchen L, roughly divided into two-thirds and one third respectively, by a short wall.*

The front door UR, opens on to a small step that leads straight into the lounge. On the wall is an entry-phone intercom. There is also a wooden chest nearby used for storage. A woman's brightly coloured raincoat is draped across the chest.

Next, moving along the back wall, is an archway leading off to the rest of the flat. To the left of the archway stands a bookcase. On one of its shelves stand Sarah's *proudest possessions – two National Television Awards for her role as Best Actress in the soap 'Doctors and Nurses'. There is a wall clock, facing directly towards the fireplace. The clock face is of a modern design, having single marks representing the numbers instead of the traditional Roman numerals. There is a well-stocked drinks cabinet with glasses.*

On the other side of the lounge, SR, is a fireplace containing an electric fire. On its mantelpiece are silver framed photos of Sarah *and the odd one of* David *and* Sarah *together. There are also some car keys on a pink fluffy keyring. Above the mantelpiece hangs a large mirror. A hearthrug lies in front of the fire. There is also a tall window, complete with full-length drapes, facing out on to the street.*

There is a writing desk and accompanying chair. On the desk is a telephone and a golden letter opener. Other furniture and fittings in the lounge include an armchair with matching settee, an impressive TV, and a coffee table. The whole flat has a lived-in, comfortable feel about it rather than a luxurious one. Amongst various pictures hanging on the walls is a framed 'TV Times' cover, featuring SARAH *dressed as a hospital nurse in her TV role as Sister Joan Steeples.*

Stage L is the dimly lit kitchen. Halfway down its left wall is a sliding door that covers a dumb-waiter lift and accompanying pulley rope. This must be clearly visible to the audience throughout the play. The usual utilities can be seen. A small window looks out onto a brick wall. A bunch of keys hang on a wall hook.

A suitcase, a portable typewriter in its case, and an airline bag can be seen near the front door.

As the lights go down and the curtain rises we hear a recording of a lively orchestrated version of the 'Teddy Bears' Picnic'. It is nine o'clock on a cold February morning.

SARAH SEETON, *an attractive woman in her 30s and wearing a leotard, is sitting on the floor in a yoga position facing us. She is doing her morning exercise and meditation. Her eyes are closed. She is 'omming' at different volumes and frequencies. Her husband* DAVID WOODS, *slightly older, amiable and meticulous in his manner, is speaking into the telephone but finding it difficult to concentrate due to his wife's extraordinary continuous oscillations. If he could throttle her now and get away with it, he probably would!*

DAVID	(*On the phone.*) Hello? Is that the King's Hotel in Pimlico? . . . Have you got a . . . (*Checks luggage tag on case.*) . . . Mrs Hannah Van Lee staying there? I'm afraid I don't know the room number . . . Yes, I'll wait . . .
SARAH	Omm . . .
DAVID	(*On the phone.*) Hello? Mrs Van Lee? . . . You don't know me, my name is David Woods . . . The thing is I've got your suitcase . . . That's right . . . I picked it up by mistake at Heathrow last night . . . I'm terribly sorry . . .
SARAH	Omm . . . Omm . . .

DAVID	(*On the phone.*) Yes, yes I know you don't have my case, I've just been talking to British Airways, it's still at the airport . . . they're looking after it for me . . . Would you like me to send your case around by taxi? . . . No, if you want to come and collect it, it's entirely up to you . . . My address? . . . Have you got a pen? . . .
SARAH	Omm . . . Omm . . . Omm . . .
DAVID	(*On the phone.*) It's number three, (*Pronouncing both 'F's.*) Ffoulkes Mansions, Ffoulkes Gardens, that's double 'F's, by the way, in both the Ffoulkes . . . We're known as the ffolks who live at the Ffoukes . . . sorry, one of my little jokes . . .
	(SARAH *opens her eyes and groans.*)
	It's in SW7 actually . . . South Kensington. Fine, I'll see you soon and once again, I'm terribly sorry. Goodbye. (*He hangs up.*) Whoever dreamt up our address should f . . . f . . . fatally shoot themselves!
SARAH	Honestly David, I don't know how you could have been so silly. (*She gets to her feet.*)
DAVID	Well it was an easy mistake, it's identical to mine.
SARAH	You should have looked at the label. (*She picks up an elegant silk dressing gown from the settee and puts it on.*)
DAVID	It never occurred to me. I was exhausted. The flight was already two hours late. I just waited in the scrum at the carousel, saw the case, grabbed it and got the hell out of there.
SARAH	It wouldn't have happened if I'd been with you.
DAVID	Well it's all sorted out. No harm done.

SARAH   Just make sure you reimburse this poor woman's cab fare.

DAVID   I will, don't worry.

(SARAH *goes to the drinks cabinet and pours herself a large vodka in an enormous glass.* DAVID *watches her disapprovingly.*)

DAVID   Thirsty work, meditating, is it?

SARAH   (*Ignores this.*) So, how did your little holiday go? Sorry I was out when you got back last night. One of the kids in the show is getting married and threw a bash at *Stringfellows*.

DAVID   It went very well, as it happens. Six weeks in Paris and I feel like a new man.

SARAH   Six weeks anywhere and I feel like a new man. (*She laughs, he doesn't.*) Only joking.

DAVID   I've never felt better. I took a long leisurely walk along the Seine every afternoon and even managed to give up smoking.

SARAH   Again? Oh well done, darling, it'll give you something to bore people with at dinner parties. (*She pours herself another vodka.*)

DAVID   If I can give up the dreaded weed, you can surely cut down on that stuff.

SARAH   Why should I? I like it.

DAVID   At nine in the morning?

SARAH   Shh!! Don't tell my liver, it still thinks we're at *Stringfellows*. (*Knocks back her vodka.*)

DAVID   Anyway, guess what?

SARAH	What?
DAVID	I finished my book.
SARAH	It took you six weeks to read a book?
DAVID	No, no, no. I finished writing my new one.
SARAH	(*Bored.*) Oh . . .
DAVID	Well, the first draft, anyway. I said I'd do it, didn't I? I just needed the time, the space. I couldn't concentrate here with the pressure of work and everything.
SARAH	David, you're an accountant. Main qualification being able to add. It's hardly a Cabinet post. Now where is my nail file? (*She exits through the archway.*)
DAVID	Be that as it may, I desperately needed the break. Not that I didn't discipline myself, because I did. (*Proudly.*) Oh yes. Six hours a day at the typewriter. Nothing but blank sheets, messy ribbons, aching wrists but I did it.
	(SARAH *returns filing her nails.*)
SARAH	Sorry, what were you saying? Six hours a day, aching wrists? Doing what exactly?
DAVID	Finishing my new book. It took a big effort, I can tell you. I typed till I dropped. (*He takes the portable typewriter out of its case and admires it as he puts it on the desk.*)
SARAH	Why don't you invest in a laptop?
DAVID	You know why. Agatha Christie once owned this typewriter. Just think, she may have hammered out *Murder on the Orient Express* on these very keys. Have you noticed how the 'P' is worn

	down? (*Hits the 'P' key repeatedly.*) Poirot! Poirot!
SARAH	That typewriter was put on *eBay* by a gardener who once worked for Agatha Christie. The chances she hammered out anything on it are remote.
DAVID	Well I like to think she did.
SARAH	So what's this blockbuster called?
DAVID	Er . . . well I haven't quite settled on the final title yet.
SARAH	Well, what's it about then?
DAVID	Best I don't tell you, darling. It'll ruin your surprise when you read it.
SARAH	Oh for goodness sake, anyone would think you'd written some Booker Prize, not another crummy never-to-be-published detective novel. Where have you put it? In here? (*She opens his airline bag and takes out a thick, typed manuscript held together by a bulldog clip.*) Now, let's have a look.
DAVID	No! I don't want you to look at it. Not yet.
	(*He tries to get it off her but she teases him with it by just keeping it out of his reach.*)
SARAH	Why ever not? I'm always the first to read your novels. And usually the last.
DAVID	Yes, but this one isn't quite ready yet, Sarah. It still needs a bit of work. You'll be the first, I promise you. Please?
	(*She hands the manuscript over to him.*)

SARAH	You know your trouble, you can't stand criticism.
DAVID	That's not true. I don't mind criticism if it's constructive.
SARAH	I am constructive.
DAVID	I'm afraid "absurd plot, terrible characters, crap dialogue" is not my idea of being constructive.
SARAH	That was your first one, *Murder and Money add up to Death,* or whatever it was called.
DAVID	*Money plus Motive add up to Murder* was my second one, Sarah. *A Husband minus a Wife equals Death* was the first. As well you know.
SARAH	Oh yes . . . Both terrible titles. You can tell they were written by an accountant. (*She refills her glass.*)
	(DAVID *puts the manuscript in the desk drawer and locks it, putting the key in his pocket.*)
DAVID	You may scoff, but I've a sneaky feeling this may be the one that gets published. Third time lucky and all that.
SARAH	I don't know why you're so hell-bent on producing a best seller. I earn more than enough to keep the wolf from our door. The show's doing well in the ratings and I've just signed my new contract. Good nosh and drinkies for at least three more years. (*She raises her glass to him and knocks back another vodka.*)
DAVID	Yes but it would be nice not to be known as *Mr Sarah Seeton* for once.
SARAH	I'll earn it, you invest it.

DAVID   I do have talent, Sarah.

SARAH   Of course you do, darling.

                (*The front doorbell rings.*)

                That'll be my car. Keep the driver amused, will you? I won't be a minute. (*She exits through archway.*)

                (DAVID *opens the front door and finds* MRS BECK, *a woman in her 50s, standing there. She's holding some letters. She wears a utility belt around her middle. Its pouches are packed with screwdrivers, wrench, a small hammer, etc. Some pouches are kept empty to put small ornaments into for* MRS BECK *is a kleptomaniac. Whenever she's not being observed objects will often disappear into her belt.*)

MRS BECK   (*Looking at him coldly.*) Ah, you're back then. (*She enters the flat walking slowly and bent because of her bad back.*)

DAVID   No, I'm still in Paris.

MRS BECK   Eh?

DAVID   You're looking at a hologram, Mrs Beck.

MRS BECK   (*Baffled.*) A hollow what? What are you talking about?

DAVID   Oh, forget it.

MRS BECK   (*Sees the portable typewriter.*) I suppose you've been writing another one of your daft books?

DAVID   Yes, as it happens.

MRS BECK   Take my advice and give it up because, let's face it, you'll never be Jeremy Archer, will you?

DAVID	Jeffrey.
MRS BECK	Eh?
DAVID	He's not Jeremy, he's Jeffrey.
MRS BECK	That's what I said.
DAVID	Oh for goodness sake, what have you got there? The post?
	(*He reaches out for the letters but* MRS BECK *doesn't hand them over.*)
MRS BECK	Nothing for you, they're all for Miss Seeton.
DAVID	Well I'll give them to her.
MRS BECK	No, I'll give them to her, if it's all the same with you.
DAVID	Oh honestly. (*Calling out.*) Sarah? It's our loveable old chirpy, cockney me-old-back's-giving-me-gyp porter.
	(MRS BECK *gives* DAVID *a filthy look and then without* DAVID *seeing slips the golden letter opener, lying on the desk, into her pouch.* SARAH *comes through the archway still wearing her dressing gown.*)
SARAH	Ah, Mrs Beck.
	(*An irritated* DAVID *retreats into the kitchen and makes some coffee.*)
MRS BECK	(*All smiles.*) Brought the post up for you.
SARAH	(*Taking the letters.*) Thank you. How are you keeping?

MRS BECK   Well me old back's giving me . . . (*She stops and changes subject.*) 'Ere, I thought you were very good in *Doctors and Nurses* on the box last night.

SARAH   Well thank you.

MRS BECK   I er . . . I don't suppose you could have a word with that dishy Doctor Richard? I'm having me usual problems.

SARAH   Mrs Beck . . .

MRS BECK   Only my GP hasn't a clue when it comes to anything of a physical nature. He's more your mind-over-matter type.

SARAH   Yes, but . . .

MRS BECK   And backs can be slippery customers you know.

SARAH   Mrs Beck, we're actors playing roles. It's not a real hospital.

MRS BECK   Oh I realise that. I'm not stupid.

DAVID   (*From kitchen.*) Oh no . . .

MRS BECK   . . . But you must pick up a bit of medical whatsit along the way. And that Doctor Richard has such a nice voice.

SARAH   Well yes . . .

MRS BECK   And hair.

SARAH   I suppose so but . . .

MRS BECK   And hands. His hands could get to grips with my old back, no problem. I'll tell you what, if he wants to come round one evening and

	have one of my fish suppers, he'd be more than welcome.
Sarah	(*Humouring her.*) Yes, well I'll find out if he knows anything about *backs* and get *back* to you.
Mrs Beck	See what you did there. Many thanks, dear. Cheerio then.
Sarah	Bye.
Mrs Beck	Bye.
	(*There is a moment of silence.*)
Mrs Beck	Right, well I'll be off then. (*Muttering to herself.*) You'd think if someone brought the mail up, they'd be offered a cup of tea but oh no . . . far too much trouble . . .
	(Mrs Beck *shuffles off into the hallway.* David *comes into the lounge with his coffee. He sits down.*)
David	Daft old bat!
Sarah	It hasn't been easy for her since her husband died. She's had to take over all his jobs.
David	Can't see the point in having a porter with a bad back. It's like having a footballer with only one leg.
Sarah	I think you're being very unfair, David. Anyway, where would she live? You know how she loves her little flat. (*Goes to pick up the golden letter opener off the desk and is puzzled it's not there.*) That's funny . . . where's my new letter opener?

(The phone rings. SARAH puts her letters down on the desk and answers it.)

SARAH (*On the phone.*) Hello? . . . speaking . . . he's what . . . Well can't he get it fixed? . . . Oh I see . . . Can you send another? . . . They're all busy? . . . Uh-huh . . . Typical . . . Who? . . . Oh, I suppose so . . . Okay bye . . . (*She replaces the phone.*)

DAVID Who was that?

SARAH Production office. My driver's broken down on the Shepherd's Bush roundabout. Mind you, I'm not surprised, the wreck they've been sending me lately. Its engine always sounds like a death rattle.

DAVID Well I can't drive you in, darling. I have to wait for this suitcase woman; and then I'm going to put a few hours in at the office. Catch up on work. (*He picks up the pink fluffy keyring and car keys off the mantelpiece.*) Why not drive yourself in? Oh you can't, can you? I'd forgotten, you've just drunk a *gallon of vodka*. (*Returns the keys to the mantelpiece.*)

SARAH Don't worry, your brother's going to pick me up. It's on his way. They just caught him.

DAVID Robert? Oh good, I haven't seen him for ages.

SARAH It won't be a social call, David, our rehearsals start at ten.

DAVID All right, all right. No harm in a couple of minutes' chinwag, surely?

(A pause.)

SARAH You realise I'm going to kill Robert tomorrow, don't you?

DAVID	(*Chokes on his coffee.*) YOU'RE GOING TO WHAT??
SARAH	We're filming the 'murder at the wedding' scene in the morning. Your poor brother finally gets the bullet. Literally. (*She shapes her fingers like a gun and mimes shooting him.*) Sister Steeples shoots the randy radiographer dead.
DAVID	So you finally got your way and Robert's to be written out?
SARAH	Yep.
DAVID	But do you have to have him killed off? He'll never be able to return. Couldn't he just be seen doing the taxi ride of shame through the hospital gates like everyone else?
	(*She checks her appearance in the mirror.*)
SARAH	No. The show's better off without him.
	(*Sees DAVID's disapproving look.*)
	I am the original star of *Doctors and Nurses*, David. The producers occasionally listen to my point of view.
DAVID	I still can't believe you've done it.
	(*She puts on a huge wig and arranges it facing the mirror.*)
SARAH	I'm sorry, I know he's your brother but I will not have a screen husband who wears a wig. It's not good for my image.
DAVID	Robert's been wearing that wig in the show for seven years. You never complained before.

SARAH	I've nothing against wigs. Loads of actors in the show wear them and fortunately the public have no idea. Your brother's big mistake was being photographed *without* his wig. All of a sudden the hunk I'm marrying ages twenty years and I'm exchanging vows with Mr Magoo.
DAVID	But Robert always takes it off when he goes swimming. Personally, I think someone tipped off that newspaper. Someone who works at his health club probably. I don't trust that changing room attendant, the one with the towels . . . what's-his-name?
SARAH	(*Lustily.*) Jean-Pierre.
DAVID	Yes, Jean-Pierre. Too full of himself by half.
SARAH	Whatever, he should have been more careful.
	(*The intercom buzzes.*)
	Talk of the devil. Let him in will you. I won't be a tick. (*She exits through the archway to change.*)
DAVID	(*He stamps his feet to attention.*) YES SIR!! (*Into intercom.*) Hello?
SARAH	(*Off.*) Is it him?
ROBERT	(*On intercom.*) David? It's me, Robert. Shall I come up or wait in the car?
DAVID	(*To* SARAH.) Yes, it's . . .
SARAH	(*Off.*) Is it your brother?
DAVID	(*To* SARAH.) Yes. (Into intercom.) Why don't you . . .
SARAH	(*Off.*) Is it *him?*

DAVID	(*To* SARAH.) Yes. (*Into intercom.*) No, come up. (*He presses the buzzer.*)
SARAH	(*Off.*) Is it Robert, David?
DAVID	YES!! (*He picks up his own coffee cup and* SARAH'S *empty glass and takes them into the kitchen.*)
	(*The front doorbell rings.* DAVID *opens the door.* ROBERT WOODS, DAVID'S *younger brother, enters. He is in his 30s and keeps himself in good shape, regularly working out. He's wearing his wig.*)
DAVID	Hello, Robert.
ROBERT	David. How was gay Paris?
DAVID	Not bad, actually. I feel like a million dollars and far more important, I finished my new book.
ROBERT	Well done.
DAVID	It wasn't easy. I had to discipline myself. Blank sheets, messy ribbons, aching wrists but I did it.
ROBERT	I'll look forward to reading it. I really enjoyed the last one, *Death plus a Murdered Husband equals Money.*
DAVID	(*Coldly.*) No, no. *A Husband minus a Murder adds up to a Wife.* What? (*Confused.*) No! (*Thinks again.*) *Money plus Motive add up to Murder.* Yes, *Money plus Motive add up to Murder.* That was the last one.
ROBERT	Right, I knew it was some sort of algebraic equation. Well, let's hope this one gets into print. (*He hits the 'P' key on the typewriter.*) Poirot!

DAVID   It'll get into print all right. (*Lowering his voice.*) This is the book, Robert.

ROBERT   The book? (*Realising the implication.*) Oh, you mean *the* book!

              (DAVID *nods "Yes" and is about to elaborate when* SARAH *enters through the archway dressed for the day. Her eyes are fixed on* ROBERT'S *wig. It obviously annoys her to the extreme.*)

SARAH   Good morning, Robert.

ROBERT   Sarah.

SARAH   All ready for your last rehearsal?

ROBERT   You bet. I've been up half the night learning my lines. Not going to risk any fluffs on my last day.

SARAH   Good. Robert, why do you insist on continuing to wear that dead animal on your head when the whole world now knows you're as bald as a coot?

              (*She tries to lift his wig off but he stops her.*)

ROBERT   Oww!!! Do you mind? I happen to very attached to my rug.

              (SARAH *picks up her raincoat lying on the wooden chest and puts it on.*)

SARAH   Obviously. (*To* DAVID.) I'll see you this evening then darling. I'll tell you what, why don't I call round at your office and you can take me out to eat at the Ivy or somewhere? Celebrate your return.

DAVID   (*With little enthusiasm.*) All right, could do, I suppose.

SARAH	See you about six-thirty then?
DAVID	Fine.
	(SARAH *offers her cheek for* DAVID *to kiss goodbye but he ignores her. She quickly exits through the front door.*)
ROBERT	Bye, David.
DAVID	Oh, Robert . . .
ROBERT	Yes?
DAVID	That little discussion we had before I went to Paris.
ROBERT	Er . . . Yes?
DAVID	I have decided. Today. This afternoon.
ROBERT	(*Aghast.*) TODAY?? I can't!
DAVID	You must.
ROBERT	No . . .
DAVID	Yes!
	(SARAH *shouts from the hallway.*)
SARAH	(*Off.*) COME ON, ROBERT!!
ROBERT	Coming.
DAVID	Shall we say about five o'clock?
	(*He picks up the pink fluffy key ring from the mantelpiece and tosses it to* ROBERT, *who catches it and puts it in his pocket.*)
	Red Mercedes. It's in the usual place.

(ROBERT *looks terrified and exits.* DAVID *goes into the kitchen and returns with a brown cardboard box. He goes over to the mantelpiece and, as quickly as possible, picks up the various silver framed photographs and chucks them into the box. He then picks up the two acting awards and bungs them in the box too.*

'The Teddy Bears' Picnic' plays as the lights fade to black.

End of Scene One.)

Scene Two

It is fifteen minutes later. The room is now bare of any evidence that SARAH *lives there. The intercom buzzes.* DAVID *comes out of the kitchen and answers it.*

DAVID   (*Into intercom.*) Yes? . . .

HANNAH   (*On intercom.*) Mr Woods? Hannah Van Lee.

DAVID   (*Into intercom.*) Right. Come up, first floor.

(DAVID *straightens the furniture a bit. He notices a TV script lying on the coffee table and slings it into the waste paper basket by the desk.*

The front door bell rings. He opens the door. HANNAH *Van Lee stands there. She's in her 20s and speaks with an accent. She carries a shoulder bag.*)

HANNAH   Mr Woods?

DAVID   Yes. Please come in, Mrs Van Lee.

(HANNAH *enters the flat, very much on her guard. She appears cautious and nervous at the unfamiliar surroundings.* David *picks up the suitcase and hands it to her.*)

DAVID As I said on the phone, I picked it up by mistake off the luggage carousel. It's identical to mine. Terribly sorry.

HANNAH Don't apologise, it could have happened to anyone.

DAVID So, you were on the same flight as me from Paris?

HANNAH Yes.

DAVID Do I detect a slight accent? Australian perhaps? South African? Birmingham?

HANNAH Oh dear, is it that obvious? Yes, I come from Umzimvubu.

DAVID (*None the wiser.*) Umzimvubu?

HANNAH Umzimvubu. South Africa. It's near Durban.

DAVID Really? Look, I must give you some money for your taxi. (*He gets his wallet out.*)

HANNAH No, please, there's no need.

DAVID Are you sure?

HANNAH Positive.

DAVID Well, as you wish.

HANNAH I'm just grateful to get my case back. (*She opens the front door to leave.*)

DAVID I thought you would be. The funny thing is I can't understand why you didn't tell the airline

	staff that your case had gone missing. (*He closes the front door.*)
HANNAH	What . . . what are you doing?
DAVID	You see I was curious, very curious, when I learned that you *hadn't* reported your lost case to the airline. It seemed very odd, to say the least.
	(HANNAH *stares at* DAVID.)
DAVID	In fact, I became so intrigued that I decided there could only be one reason. That Mrs Van Lee had something *in* her case that she didn't want anyone to know about.
HANNAH	Where are they?
DAVID	. . . And curiosity got the better of me.
HANNAH	Where are they?
DAVID	. . . So I did something I normally wouldn't dream of doing.
HANNAH	I asked you a question.
DAVID	. . . I picked the lock. (*He holds up a small talcum powder tin.*) And what should I find cleverly hidden inside this but diamonds, no less!
	(DAVID *produces a small, soft suede bag with a string-pull top out of his pocket and empties some diamonds onto the coffee table.* HANNAH *grabs them.*)
HANNAH	Some are missing.
DAVID	I know. Three to be precise. Here's one of them.

(DAVID *takes a handkerchief out of his pocket and empties a blue coloured diamond on to the table.* HANNAH *immediately grabs it.*)

DAVID I've never seen a diamond that blue colour before. Is it particularly valuable?

HANNAH Not particularly. (*She drops all the diamonds into the suede bag and places it inside her own bag.*) Where are the others?

DAVID How much are they worth?

HANNAH Not a lot, er . . . a few hundred pounds perhaps.

DAVID Each?

HANNAH No. All together. All of them.

DAVID Oh come on, they must be worth more than that. You've taken quite a risk.

HANNAH All right, so they're worth a bit more. But you have to know where to sell them.

DAVID And you do?

HANNAH I have a contact.

DAVID Which would imply that you have done this sort of thing before.

(HANNAH *says nothing.*)

Come on, Mrs Van Lee, time to spill the beans, lay it on the line, put your cards on the table.

(HANNAH *stares at him, not sure whether to trust him.*)

	Let the cat out of the bag, get it off your chest, reveal your secret.
	(HANNAH *is still not sure what to do.*)
	Take the weight off your shoulders, put up your hand, admit that . . .
HANNAH	(*Can take no more.*) All right, all right!! But if I tell you, do you promise you'll keep it to yourself?
DAVID	Scout's honour.
HANNAH	All right then. Back home in Umzimvubu . . .
DAVID	Umzimvubu, yes, yes we've done that bit.
HANNAH	. . . my husband works in a jeweller's. One day he was alone in the shop and he faked a robbery . . .
DAVID	Aha! No wonder you smuggled them into this country.
HANNAH	But you don't understand. We've never done this sort of thing before. We need the money for our son's medical treatment. Little Timmy's desperately ill with . . . with . . .
DAVID	With? With what?
HANNAH	With some desperate illness. They're having difficulty diagnosing it.
DAVID	Who are?
HANNAH	The doctors, the specialists.
DAVID	What doctors? What specialists?
HANNAH	At the hospital.
DAVID	What hospital?

HANNAH	The . . . The Desmond Tutu Children's Hospital in er . . . Johannesburg.

(*A pause.*)

DAVID	(*Incredulous.*) I don't believe a word of it. Desperate illnesses? Little Timmy? The Desmond Tutu Children's Hospital in Johannesburg? It's just not adding up, not adding up at all.
HANNAH	It's true.
DAVID	Codswallop!! You're just an ordinary common-or-garden diamond smuggler, aren't you, Mrs Van Lee?

(*A pause.*)

HANNAH	Er . . . Yes.
DAVID	I thought as much.
HANNAH	Look, just give them back and let me sell them. I'll see you're all right.
DAVID	Cut me in, you mean?
HANNAH	You haven't already sold them, have you?
DAVID	Don't worry, they're quite safe. And you can have them back. Provided you do a little favour for me.

(HANNAH *looks puzzled.*)

Let me elaborate.

(DAVID *opens his airline bag and takes out a small video camera with a flip-out screen. He hands it to her.*)

DAVID	Can you work one of these?
HANNAH	(*Examines camera.*) I should think so. Why?
DAVID	I want you to make a film for me. In return for your remaining two diamonds.
HANNAH	What sort of film?
DAVID	A film of my wife. At it.
HANNAH	At it? At what?
DAVID	Do I have to spell it out?
	(HANNAH *looks puzzled.*)
DAVID	Oh for goodness sake! My wife is having an affair and I want you to film it.
HANNAH	What? Why do you want me to film it?
DAVID	For a divorce. Look, she thinks I don't know about her little indiscretions, if you can call them little. Twice a week in this very flat. And always when I'm at work.
HANNAH	If you're not here, how do you know she's having an affair?
DAVID	One afternoon she phoned me to make sure the coast was clear and didn't replace the handset correctly. I could hear my wife mixing her lover double gin and tonics before he started giving her triple orgasms.
HANNAH	Why don't you just hire some private eye to photograph them?
DAVID	I would prefer to do it this way, if you don't mind. I want something more tangible, more concrete. Six grainy ten-by-eights of my wife

	entering the building with lover boy waving his white stick do not necessarily prove that she's committed adultery. On the other hand, a video film will. I want first class evidence, Mrs Van Lee. (*With a slight smile.*) Naked truth, if you like.
HANNAH	If you're some kind of weirdo who wants to get off watching his wife with another man . . .
DAVID	I'm not! But even if I was I don't think you're in any position to turn my request down.
	(*A pause.*)
HANNAH	Why don't you just discreetly set the camera up and leave it recording? You don't need me.
DAVID	I need your assistance in focusing it and framing it. Just make the film of my wife and her lover and I'll give you your diamonds back.
	(HANNAH *considers the proposition for a moment.*)
HANNAH	All right. When?
DAVID	If we go by her recent timetable, and my wife is nothing if not predictable, any time from five this afternoon. She's already made sure I'll be waiting for her at my office in Covent Garden.
HANNAH	Okay, so where's the bedroom?
DAVID	No, she would never use the bed. Too risky. Strange aftershave on the pillow, stains on the sheets. No, I'm reasonably certain that she entertains him in *here*.
HANNAH	How can you be sure?
DAVID	Well for one thing we only have one telephone, (*He points at it.*), and I could hear their pleasure

only too clearly. My guess is on the settee or perhaps on the rug in front of the fire. My wife was always romantic about making love in front of the fire. At least she was when we first married. Don't ask me why. Probably saw Hugh Grant get his arse roasted in a film once.

HANNAH So where do I film from?

(*Holding the video camera,* HANNAH *looks for a suitable hiding place. She decides to go into the kitchen.* DAVID *promptly follows her. She stops by the dumb-waiter door.*)

HANNAH What's this?

DAVID That's the dumb-waiter.

HANNAH Dumb-waiter?

(DAVID *slides open the dumb-waiter door. A large, empty black dustbin is in the compartment.*)

DAVID Rather quaint name for an old fashioned waste-disposer. You put your rubbish in the bin and pull this rope, (*He points to the pulley rope.*) and it takes it straight down to the basement car park. Every flat has one and if you're lucky Mrs Beck, our back-troubled porter, empties all eight on a Friday. (*He lifts the dustbin out and puts it in a corner of the kitchen.*)

HANNAH I could hide in there. It gives a direct line of vision.

DAVID A bit dirty isn't it?

(*She sticks her head into the compartment and quickly withdraws it.*)

HANNAH You're telling me!

(DAVID *slides the dumb-waiter door shut. They come back into the lounge looking for another hiding place.*)

DAVID   You must be totally concealed.

(HANNAH *walks up to the wooden chest.*)

HANNAH What about this?

DAVID   No, it's not tall enough . . . Oh, you mean *inside* it?

HANNAH Is it big enough?

DAVID   Possibly. It belonged to my grandfather. We used to hide in it when we were children. Let's clear the junk out . . .

(*He opens the lid and removes an umbrella, a battered tennis racket, ice skates.*)

There we go, try it for size . . .

(HANNAH *puts her bag down and climbs into the chest, crouching down inside it.* DAVID *closes the lid on top of her. Then, in a split second as he talks, he opens her bag and searches for the suede bag inside.*)

DAVID   Any good? You should be able to cover practically every angle in the room.

(*Still searching the bag, he places his knee on top of the chest to keep her in there.*)

HANNAH (*Inside chest.*) Mr Woods? What are you doing? I need to look through the gap.

DAVID   (*Frantically searching the bag.*) It's stuck.

HANNAH	(*Banging on inside of chest.*) Mr Woods!! Mr Woods!!
	(*To his great relief, he finds the suede bag, takes out the blue diamond using a handkerchief and puts it in his pocket. He then puts her bag back on the floor. He removes his knee from the chest.*)
DAVID	(*Bangs the lock with his fist.*) Sorry about that, it's the catch. I'll oil it later. (*He opens the lid.*)
HANNAH	(*Climbing out of chest and giving* DAVID *a strange look.*) See that you do. How long will I be in there?
DAVID	Not long. As I said before, we've arranged to meet about half past six.
	(HANNAH *looks through the video camera eyepiece, sizing up angles, direction, etc.*)
DAVID	Just make sure you get them both in the frame. I don't want any heads cut off!
HANNAH	Don't worry. Now what happens after they've gone? When do I get the diamonds?
	(DAVID *takes a mobile phone out of his pocket and throws it to* HANNAH *who catches it.*)
DAVID	Use that, I bought it in Paris. It's pre-paid and has one number programmed in on speed-dial. My office direct line. As soon as I hear from you, I'll come straight back. It takes about twenty-five minutes. No, make that longer, rush hour. I'll check the video recording and as long as my wife and rogering Romeo are on it, you get your diamonds. Meanwhile my wife will have made the opposite journey and be looking for me at my office.

(HANNAH *puts the mobile phone in her bag.*)

HANNAH The only reason I'm doing this ridiculous charade is because I must have those stones. I'm meeting my contact in the morning. I must have those diamonds!

DAVID You'll get them, don't worry.

(*She walks to the front door to leave but then turns.*)

HANNAH Oh, one little detail you forget.

DAVID Oh?

HANNAH How do I get in?

DAVID Of course. (*He walks into the kitchen and takes a bunch of keys off a hook on the wall.*) Our spare ones.

(*He hands them to her. She puts the keys in her bag. She then picks up her suitcase and opens the front door.*)

HANNAH I'll be back later then.

DAVID That's right. Look, don't appear so hard done by. I'm not asking you to do anything dangerous. I just want the film made. (*Laughs.*) There's no need to scowl like Sister Steeples.

HANNAH Who?

DAVID Joan Steeples. The sexy nurse with the permanent frown and the temporary husbands in *Doctors and Nurses*.

(HANNAH *looks blank.*)

DAVID	The TV series? Oh, I don't suppose you get it in South Africa.
HANNAH	*Doctors in Nurses?* No, I don't think so.
DAVID	No! Not *Doctors in Nurses*, *Doctors and Nurses*.
HANNAH	*Doctors and Nurses*. No . . .
DAVID	She's played by that actress, oh what's she called . . . er . . . Sarah . . . Sarah Seeton. That's right, Sarah Seeton. She's a big star over here. Huge.
HANNAH	Well I've never heard of her. Goodbye, Mr Woods.
	(HANNAH *exits through the front door.* DAVID *closes it behind her and then goes into the kitchen. He returns carrying the brown cardboard box and and quickly walks around the lounge returning the photos and awards to their original positions starting with the framed 'TV Times' cover on the wall. As he does this, he absent-mindedly sings and hums . . .*)
DAVID	(*Sings.*) "If you go down to the *Woods* today You're sure of a big surprise. If you go down to the *Woods* today, You'll never believe your eyes La, la, la, la, la, la . . . "
	(*The lively orchestrated music of the 'Teddy Bears' Picnic' builds as the lights fade to blackout.*
	End of Scene Two.)

Scene Three.

It's 4.30 that afternoon. The flat is empty, lights out. HANNAH *unlocks the front door and lets herself in, relocking the door behind her. She's dressed in black, wearing gloves and a black beanie. She stands there for a few seconds thinking.*

After a moment she walks over to the wooden chest and opens the lid. She takes the video camera out of her bag and looks around the room sizing up angles, etc.

Suddenly voices are heard in the hallway outside. HANNAH *quickly climbs into the wooden chest and pulls the lid down on top of her just at the moment the front door opens.*

SARAH *enters dressed, as in Scene One, in her raincoat. She has obviously enjoyed a liquid lunch and is more than a little merry. She calls out into the flat.*

SARAH	Hello? . . . Anyone at home? . . . David? . . . (*Hearing no reply, she then speaks to someone behind her waiting in the hallway.*) The coast is clear. Come on, lover boy!! (*She switches on the light.*)
	(ROBERT *enters. He's dressed as before in Scene One and carrying a battered old case.*)
ROBERT	Probably just as well, considering what we're going to get up to. (*He quickly takes his trouser belt off and cracks it on the floor like a whip.*)
SARAH	(*Loving it.*) All right!!!
	(SARAH *removes her raincoat and casually drops it down on top of the wooden chest thus preventing any chance of* HANNAH *filming anything.* ROBERT *takes his coat off and puts it on the chair.*)
ROBERT	Now, where do you fancy? In here?

SARAH	You name it, I'm on it! Let me switch the fire on. (*She bends down to turn on the electric fire.*)
ROBERT	I'll soon warm you up.
	(*He immediately undoes his trousers. They fall to his ankles and we see his underpants. He moves in on* SARAH *and starts kissing her.*)
SARAH	Ooh!! Steady, tiger! (*Breaks from him.*) What we need is another drink or two. I refuse to do anything until we've each had a large G and T.
ROBERT	But . . .
SARAH	No buts, Robert, (*She whacks his behind.*), well maybe one. Get the ice.
ROBERT	Ice?
SARAH	Ice. (*She starts to pour the drinks.*)
ROBERT	Okay. (*He reluctantly goes towards the kitchen but his trousers cause him to trip.*) Blast!!
SARAH	Here, I'll get it. What are you like?
	(*She exits into the kitchen.* ROBERT *pulls his trousers back up. His demeanour immediately changes to a serious one as he surveys the room.*
	SARAH *returns from the kitchen carrying the ice-tray. She notices* ROBERT'S *pulled his trousers up.*)
SARAH	(*Disappointed.*) Oh . . .
	(SARAH *drops some ice-cubes into the glasses and hands* ROBERT *his drink.*)
SARAH	Cheers.

ROBERT	Cheers.
SARAH	Here's to tomorrow.
ROBERT	Yes, tomorrow. (*He takes a sip of his drink.*) Talking of which, darling . . . let's play *Doctors and Nurses*.
SARAH	I'm all for that.
	(*They kiss. He suddenly breaks from her and brings out two scripts from inside his bag.*)
ROBERT	I've got the scripts right here.
SARAH	What??
ROBERT	Just a quick rehearsal.
SARAH	Oh no, Robert, I don't want to rehearse. If we don't know the thing by now we never will.
ROBERT	Won't take a minute. I just want to run through a few of the moves we didn't get round to today. That stupid director spent so much time on those dotty bridesmaids turning up at the wrong register office sub-plot . . .
SARAH	Stage school wannabees!
ROBERT	. . . that she didn't really get round to my bit.
SARAH	*Our* bit.
ROBERT	Our bit then. I mean, this is my final scene Sarah. More people will be watching than ever. I want to go out with a bang!
SARAH	You're certainly going to do that. I shoot you in the head.

ROBERT   You know what I mean. You never know who might be watching. I want to make an impression.

SARAH   I can't see that it matters. The only TV you're going to be on in the next five years are celebrity has-been shows. Brush up on your tango in the jungle big brother!!

ROBERT   (*Ignores this.*) Now, let's see. (*He starts flicking through the script and finds the appropriate page.*) Oh, yes, I shoot you first because I'm in a jealous rage. (*Imagines this.*) Jealous rage!! (*Looks back at script.*) I think you're having an affair with my step-father's separated-at-birth identical twin Tony, who just came out of a coma, don't I?

SARAH   Ridiculous idea. Not my type at all. The man wears a ponytail. Almost as bad as your wig. (*She stares at his wig, which is beginning to irritate her.*)

ROBERT   Then I shoot you in the chest . . .

SARAH   Maybe I should shoot your wig off first? I mean the whole world knows you wear one now. It'd get me a huge laugh.

           (*She tries to rip the wig off his head but he manages to stop her.*)

ROBERT   Owww!! I wish you wouldn't do that.

SARAH   I'll catch you unawares one day.

ROBERT   Look, this scene could be really exciting. Let's lift it off the page, see what we can do with it.

SARAH   If we must.

ROBERT	(*Hands her the script.*) I just want things right for tomorrow. This episode is very important to me. You never know, it may be my last telly for years.
SARAH	Okay, okay. (*Occasionally glancing at the script, she stands up and mimes the action.*) It's my wedding day. All the guests are arriving. I'm going up the steps of the register office wearing my smart hat and that two-thousand-pound outfit I conned wardrobe into buying. You're waiting there in your Moss Bros special and your buttonhole. You put your arms out to welcome me and then . . . (*Makes a gun shape with her fingers.*) I shoot you dead on the spot. Bang! Bang! Bang! Three bullets.
ROBERT	No, no, no – you've got it back to front. I shoot you first. I've just told you that.
SARAH	Do you? (*Looks at script.*) Oh yes.
ROBERT	I hit you in the chest. That's how they get you into intensive care for three episodes. Sister Steeples being cared for by her own staff.
SARAH	That'll be the day, they hate my guts.
ROBERT	Right, let's try it again. With props this time.
SARAH	Props?
ROBERT	One of the floor managers kindly lent me a few things. (*He delves into his case and brings out a revolver.*) There's your gun. (*He aims the gun into the air and pulls the trigger a couple of times. It clicks both times.*)
SARAH	Well I hope it's louder than that tomorrow.
ROBERT	Oh, they'll put a blank in it, no doubt.
	(*He hands the gun to* SARAH.)

ROBERT	Now what else have we got? (*He delves back into his case.*)
SARAH	You didn't have to go to all this trouble.
ROBERT	Ah, your hat!
	(*He produces a large flamboyant hat and passes it to* SARAH.)
SARAH	If I wear this, I'll block out the arc lights! (*She puts it on.*) I'll have a word with wardrobe first thing in the morning.
ROBERT	My top hat. (*He puts it on. It's too big and falls down over his eyes.*)
SARAH	You look like the Artful Dodger!
ROBERT	Do I?
SARAH	Yes, quite ridiculous.
ROBERT	Hides my rug, though, doesn't it?
SARAH	I suppose it does. What else have you got in there?
ROBERT	(*Looking into the case.*) That's it. Oh, except for my gun. (*He takes out a revolver, identical to the first.*) Right . . .
SARAH	Here we go then. All set for Robert Woods' final scene. Five million people tune in as his bride gives him the one big bang that he didn't expect on his wedding day.
	(*They take their positions.*)
ROBERT	So I'm waiting on the steps, looking at my watch trying to decide if I'm doing the right thing.

SARAH	Which quite obviously you're not, being thirty seconds from a most violent death.
ROBERT	And you come running up the steps . . .
SARAH	*Walking* up the steps. This is my fourth marriage, remember?
ROBERT	Walking up the steps. You think I'm going to greet you when I suddenly pull out my gun and bang! I shoot you in the chest . . .
	(*He aims the gun and pulls the trigger. It clicks.* SARAH *collapses on the rug feigning great pain in her chest.*)
SARAH	Aaahhh!!! (*Pulls her trigger.*) And I go Bang! Bang! Bang!
	(*The gun clicks each time.* ROBERT *raises his hand to his forehead in mime as if he's been shot.*)
ROBERT	Aaahhh!!! And then I collapse on the ground, dead as a dodo. (*He collapses.*)
SARAH	Don't overdo the dead bit. They'll need my close-up reaction.
ROBERT	Should I fall on my left side or my right?
SARAH	Who cares? They'll be rolling the credits over me anyway.
ROBERT	No, no, dear, apparently the credits are going to run over the rain washing my blood down the steps.
SARAH	Ugh! Well if it's going to be raining . . . (*She walks over to the wooden chest, picks her raincoat up and puts it on.*) That's better. Don't I look fabulous in this?

ROBERT	Smashing!
SARAH	Right, from the top. With words.
	(*Unseen by* SARAH *or* ROBERT, *the lid of the wooden chest opens a fraction to allow* HANNAH *to film. Suddenly* ROBERT *puts his hands on his hips and starts taking in deep breaths.* SARAH *looks on in amazement.*)
SARAH	What on earth are you doing?
ROBERT	(*Releasing a big breath.*) I'm preparing!
SARAH	Oh for goodness sake!!
	(ROBERT *takes more deep breaths. He closes his eyes and concentrates.*)
ROBERT	Oscar, Oscar, Oscar.
SARAH	(*Bored.*) Wanker, wanker, wanker.
	(ROBERT *'finds' his motivation and lets out a big breath. He's now ready.*)
ROBERT	Okay. (*Aiming his gun at her.*) "I know about you and Tony." (*He pulls the trigger. It clicks.*)
SARAH	(*Collapsing on rug and feigning great pain in her chest.*) "Aaahhh!!!"
	(*Simultaneously* SARAH *fires back at him but to her horror a loud shot goes off and* ROBERT *falls to the ground clutching his forehead as blood pours down his face.*)
SARAH	OH MY GOD!! ROBERT! ROBERT!
	(SARAH, *completely stunned, moves towards him not believing what has happened. Suddenly he looks up at her and smiles. She jumps out of her skin.*)

ROBERT	And this is the best bit. The bit where I kill *you*.
SARAH	But . . . But you don't kill *me*, I kill *you* . . .
ROBERT	(*Getting to his feet.*) Slight rewrite, Sarah. You should have checked your gun. The blank was already in it.
SARAH	What??
ROBERT	(*Removing his top hat.*) I knew it was you who tipped off the papers about my rug.
SARAH	Your rug??
ROBERT	I haven't spent all my professional life walking around with a dead ferret balanced on top of my head just so that you could do as you please with me.

(*He points his gun at* SARAH. *She puts her hands up in front of her face.*)

SARAH	What . . . What are you doing, Robert? (*Screaming.*) Stop it!! Stop it!! I'll tell the press I love bald men.
ROBERT	Too late . . .
SARAH	I'll pay for the best hair transplant money can buy!
ROBERT	Sorry . . .
SARAH	I'LL INTRODUCE YOU TO ELTON JOHN!!!

(*A pause as* ROBERT *considers this.*)

ROBERT	No! Too late.

(SARAH *aims her gun straight at him and fires. It clicks. In sheer fear she starts walking backwards away from him. He follows her*

*pointing his gun at her. She dodges to the left
and right and then grabs his arm with the gun.
It goes off with a loud crack but the bullet
misses her and hits the wall causing the framed
'TV Times' cover to crash to the ground.* ROBERT
dispenses with the gun and grabs SARAH's *head
smashing it down on the coffee table with an
almighty thud. Her body falls limp.*

*Total silence. The whole stage is bathed in red
light.* ROBERT *tries to catch his breath.)*

ROBERT Now that wasn't in the script, but it makes a
nice little twist.

(*The front door bell rings. He freezes.*)

MRS BECK (*Off.*) Miss Seeton? Miss Seeton? Are you all
right? It's Edith Beck. I heard some awful noises.
Is everything all right?

(*She rings the doorbell again.* ROBERT *keeps
perfectly still, his mind racing.*)

MRS BECK (*Off.*) Do you want me to get the police or
something? Miss Seeton? Miss Seeton? (*More
ringing.*) Miss Seeton?

(*The doorbell stops ringing.*)

MRS BECK (*Off.*) Perhaps I was mistaken . . .

(MRS BECK *moves away from the front door.
Heaving a sigh of relief* ROBERT *quickly places
both guns and hats back into the case. He finds
the bullet in the wall and pockets it.*)

ROBERT Let's go for a little ride, bitch . . .

(*He drags* SARAH's *body into the kitchen. He
slides open the door to the dumb-waiter.
He lifts her body and squeezes it into the*

compartment. Once she's in, he slides the door shut.

He goes to the sink and runs the tap. He wipes the fake blood off his face.

He puts on his coat and picks up his case. He cautiously opens the front door, looking left and right down the hallway. All clear. He switches off the main light and exits.

The red glow of the electric fire is now all that illuminates the room.

After a few seconds, the lid of the wooden chest slowly creaks open and HANNAH *nervously climbs out having first established the room is empty.*

She takes the mobile phone that DAVID *gave her earlier out of her bag and speed-dials him. The light from the screen illuminates her face.)*

HANNAH (*On the phone.*) Hello? Mr Woods? . . . Hannah Van Lee . . . Look you'd better . . . Yes, I started to film but something's happened . . . I can't tell you now. Just get over here right away . . . No, your wife's not here . . . she's . . . she's gone. Listen I'll meet you in the pub at the end of your street . . . Okay? I can't stay here . . . I'll tell you later. Just hurry. Please! (*She puts the phone back in her bag along with the video camera. She then quickly runs out of the flat, shutting the front door behind her.*)

(*The dumb-waiter pulley system begins to creak into action as someone pulls it from below. The pulley system makes an eerie, creaking, squeaky noise.*

Blackout.)

Scene Four

About fifty minutes later. DAVID, *dressed as in Scene Two but wearing his overcoat, comes bursting through the front door followed by a highly jittery* HANNAH. *He switches the main light on.*

DAVID	For goodness sake, pull yourself together! Did you or did you not film them?
HANNAH	Yes but . . .
DAVID	Then you've kept your side of the bargain. I suppose they were naked.
HANNAH	No, no! There was no sex, but never mind that, there were guns, an accident . . .
	(*A silence.*)
DAVID	What do you mean? What's happened to my wife?
HANNAH	She's . . . dead.
DAVID	DEAD??
	(DAVID *stares at her in horror.*)
HANNAH	They were playing some game. Role-playing, I don't know. She shot him but he wasn't really hurt and then he was going to shoot her but he missed so he attacked her by the coffee table and then I thought he was going to . . .
DAVID	NEVER MIND HIM, WHERE THE HELL IS MY WIFE??
HANNAH	(*Points towards the kitchen.*) He put her body in the garbage thing.
DAVID	(*Incredulous.*) HE PUT HER BODY IN THE GARBAGE THING??

	(DAVID *runs over to the dumb-waiter and slides open the door. The compartment is not there. He looks down the lift shaft.*)
HANNAH	You wouldn't believe this guy. He was nuts . . . Wait a minute! I've got the whole thing recorded, haven't I? (*She gets the video camera out of her bag.*)
DAVID	Don't touch that! Give it to me! (*He snatches it off her.*)
HANNAH	I don't understand. Your wife has been killed.
DAVID	That's right. Just as I planned.
	(*A pause.*)
HANNAH	I don't follow. Just as *you* planned . . .
DAVID	Or more accurately, just as *we* planned.
HANNAH	What?
	(*During the following* DAVID *flips out the mini viewing screen on the video camera and watches the recording. At no time do the audience see the screen.*)
DAVID	My brother Robert and me. We've had this murder planned for a long time. We were going to pull it off sometime in the future but then you came bumbling along from Umzimmermanbooboo and all of a sudden it was all systems go.
HANNAH	Me?
DAVID	Yes, that was the genius of the whole thing. To get someone else to murder her. And someone else again to film that murder. (*Something's

	not right on the viewing screen.) Where's the sound?? (*He holds the camera to his ear.*)
HANNAH	(*Remembering.*) Oh! I turned it off earlier when I was trying it out.
DAVID	Idiot! (*Looking back at the screen.*) Still, silent movies, even better. (*Snaps the viewing screen shut.*) You see, you have been a victim in a little scene I set up. My wife is, or maybe I should say *was*, a famous actress. Sarah Seeton. But fortunately you've never heard of her. Her fame far exceeded her talent, which even with a good script, which wasn't very often, was negligible. I decided she would be worth more to me dead than alive.

(*He puts the video camera on the desk and then picks up the framed 'TV Times' cover from the floor and shows it to her.*)

HANNAH	(*Stares at the cover.*) So that's why you asked me if I knew the TV show?
DAVID	It would have been a disaster for me if you had.
HANNAH	But why kill her?
DAVID	Why do you think? Money, isn't that always the motive? And a little bit of unavoidable fame. Oh yes, this little story is going to make front pages for quite a while, believe me. If all has gone to plan, Robert should have bundled Sarah's corpse into the boot of her car and be driving down to Hampshire at this very moment. He's going to dump her body on the edge of the New Forest where the police will eventually find it. The papers will have a field day. What was she doing there? Who killed her? It'll be the murder mystery of the decade. And I'm going to end up stinking rich but smelling of roses.

HANNAH	Life assurance?
DAVID	Credit me with some intelligence. That old routine would have been a dead giveaway so I cancelled her policy months ago. No, my gain from Sarah's murder is much more subtle.

(DAVID *takes a key from his pocket and unlocks a drawer in the desk. He takes out the thick, typed manuscript he put in there in Scene One. He passes it to* HANNAH.)

HANNAH	What's this?
DAVID	My latest unpublished book. Be careful with it. It took a lot of time and effort. Blank sheets, messy ribbons, aching wrists . . .
HANNAH	(*Reading the title page.*) "Soap plus Scandal plus Sex add up to Sarah Seeton".
DAVID	Slight departure for me really. I normally write novels but this one's a biography. A husband's tale.
HANNAH	A kiss and tell book?
DAVID	More like kiss and kill.

(HANNAH *flicks through a few pages.*)

HANNAH	Clever stuff.
DAVID	I think so.
HANNAH	The police will find your wife's body and . . .
DAVID	The story will quite naturally be sensational front-page news and after a decent mourning period, the grieved widower will offer his own modest thoughts on the subject of his traumatic marriage to the 'Star'. (*Pointing at the book.*)

	I've worked out that with serialisation and TV rights, I can net in the region of a million big ones.
HANNAH	But why kill her? Why not just write the book?
DAVID	(*Looks at her like she is mad.*) Because the dead can't sue for libel.
HANNAH	What do you mean?
DAVID	I can say anything I want about her and no one can say I'm lying. After all I was her husband. I can make up any old rubbish. Everyone knows she liked a drink but what about her crack cocaine habit? Or her on/off affair with one of the better-known members of the Royal family? Sex in hot tubs with toy boys and ambitious young actors? And actresses? No names of course, protect the guilty. After all, I don't want to be sued for libel, do I? But I've dropped enough hints to make for juicy speculation. The whole world's celebrity mad these days; they'll swallow anything. They just need to be told by someone who was *there*. It'll be a guaranteed bestseller. And all from my imagination. It's ingenious. (*He takes the manuscript off* HANNAH.) And the final piece of my celeb-jamboree jigsaw is the film you made.
HANNAH	What good is that? You can't sell it.
DAVID	Although I was quite happy to write the book, I wasn't so confident I could carry out the actual murder. Besides, it was vital to give myself an alibi. And that's where my brother Robert comes into the picture. We worked on the plan together. The idea was to split the profits fifty-fifty. But somehow I don't think he'll be asking

for his royalties when he's seen what I've got on that video.

(DAVID *returns the manuscript to the desk drawer.*)

HANNAH You're going to blackmail your own brother with the film.

DAVID My goodness, we've got a clever one here!

HANNAH But all he has to do is go to the police.

DAVID And be arrested for murder?

HANNAH And what about me? What are you going to do with me?

(DAVID *moves slowly towards her in a creepy, threatening way. Is he going to strangle her? She looks for an escape route when he suddenly stops.*)

DAVID Do with you? I'm not going to do anything with you.

(*He takes a matchbox out of his pocket and hands it to her.*)

There you are, the two remaining diamonds as promised.

HANNAH (*Looks in matchbox.*) You seem very confident I won't go to the police.

DAVID I am. You see, when you climbed inside the chest this morning, I took back that blue diamond.

(HANNAH *stares at him in amazement, dives into her bag, finds the suede bag and looks inside it. No blue diamond.*)

DAVID   I'm surprised you hadn't already discovered it missing.

HANNAH   Where the hell is it?

DAVID   Somewhere you'll never find it. It's my guarantee you won't go to the police. Because if you do, I shall tell them where it is. And when they find it, they'll discover your fingerprints on it.

               (*He quickly delves into her bag and before she can stop him fishes out the mobile phone he gave her earlier.*)

               As they will on this.

               (*She tries to grab the phone off him but he holds it just out of her reach. He then pockets it.*)

HANNAH   But that stone is worth a fortune.

DAVID   Then you should have taken better care of it, shouldn't you?

               (HANNAH *stares at him as she realises the full horror of the situation.*)

HANNAH   Why don't you just give it back to me? I did what you asked, didn't I?

DAVID   Sorry. My rules. (*He opens the front door for her.*) Goodbye.

HANNAH   But . . .

DAVID   Goodbye.

               (DAVID *indicates for her to leave.* HANNAH *realises there is no more she can say or do for now. She exits.*)

(DAVID *smiles and walks over to the drinks cabinet. He pours himself a large whisky. He knocks it back and then takes his coat off, putting it on the chair. The intercom buzzes.*)

DAVID   Now what? (*Into intercom.*) Yes?

ROOT   (*On intercom.*) Mr Woods? Police here. Could I see you for a moment?

DAVID   (*Into intercom.*) Police? What do you want?

ROOT   (*On intercom.*) It's very important. Shouldn't take a minute.

(DAVID *realises he has no choice but to let him in.*)

DAVID   (*Into intercom.*) Well . . . er . . . yes, all right. Come up. It's the first floor. (*He presses the buzzer.*)

(*Suddenly, to* DAVID'S *surprise, a noise comes from the dumb-waiter shaft. It is the creaking and squeaking of the dumb-waiter being returned from the basement.* DAVID *finds this odd and goes into the kitchen to investigate further. He approaches the dumb-waiter and slides the door open. The dead body of* ROBERT *falls halfway out of the compartment. His wig falls off. There is blood dripping from a bullet hole in his forehead.* DAVID *recoils in total horror.*)

DAVID   OH NO! ROBERT!!! ROBERT!!!

(DAVID *flies into a mad panic. He attempts to squeeze the body of* ROBERT *back into the compartment. It's a difficult job, as soon as he succeeds getting one limb in, another slips out and hangs there. During this, the doorbell rings.*

A fear-stricken DAVID *panics as he tries to stuff the body into the dumb-waiter. But it won't quite fit.*

The doorbell rings again.)

ROOT (*Off.*) Mr Woods? It's the police, can you open your door please? I'd like to talk to you.

DAVID (*Squeezing arms, legs and wig into the dumb-waiter.*) GET IN, WON'T YOU! GET IN!!

(ROOT *rings the doorbell and knocks loudly on the door.*

Blackout.

End of Act One.)

ACT TWO

Scene One

The same. The action is continuous. Root *is ringing the doorbell and knocking on the front door.*

ROOT   (*Off.*) Mr Woods? Are you in there? It's the police.

             (*To his great relief,* DAVID *finally manages to squeeze* ROBERT'S *corpse into the dumb-waiter. He slides the door shut. He then rushes to the front door, takes a deep breath and opens it to* DETECTIVE INSPECTOR ROOT *who's wearing plain clothes.* MRS BECK *stands beside him. They both enter.*)

MRS BECK   There he is, Inspector. That's him. Mr Woods. Reckons he's a writer.

ROOT   Yes, thank you, Mrs Beck.

MRS BECK   Let's see if he can write his way out of this one.

DAVID   (*To* MRS BECK.) What are you babbling on about?

MRS BECK   You'll soon find out.

ROOT   Yes, thank you, Mrs Beck. I can manage now.

MRS BECK   Oh. You're sure you won't need me?

ROOT   Quite sure.

MRS BECK   Well if you change your mind, I'll be downstairs in my flat. Number one.

ROOT   Right.

MRS BECK	I'm doing myself a nice bit of haddock if you're hungry later. With parsley sauce and new potatoes. You're welcome to join me.
ROOT	Thank you, but I've eaten.
MRS BECK	Oh, right, well I'll be off then.
ROOT	Yes.
MRS BECK	But you know where to find me if you need me.
ROOT	Yes . . .
DAVID	LOOK, JUST GET GOING, MRS BECK!!
	(MRS BECK *gives* DAVID *a filthy look and exits. Before she goes, however, she picks up the whisky glass* DAVID *recently drank from and slips it into her utility-belt pouch.* DAVID *and* ROOT *do not see this.*)
DAVID	Now, Inspector, what's all this about? It's been a while since I last saw you.
ROOT	Last summer, if I remember correctly. When your wife kindly hosted our showbiz charity auction.
DAVID	That's right, Inspector . . . Bush?
ROOT	Root!
DAVID	Of course, now what . . .
ROOT	I'll never forget that night because I won the raffle, didn't I? A week's cruising on the Norfolk Broads. Wonderful prize.
DAVID	Yes, yes, so you did.

ROOT	Unfortunately the occasion was slightly marred. There was talk of fiddling. A lot of people thought it was fixed, all those bits of paper with my name on them but your wife stood up for me. Insisted the drawer was fair. I was very grateful to her.
DAVID	I'm sure you were, but what . . .
ROOT	It was a marvellous holiday. In fact it gave me the sailing bug. I'm saving up for a motor cruiser now. That's my dream. A twin engine, six berth, forty-footer. I'm retiring at the end of the year, you know.
DAVID	This is all very interesting, but could you please get to the point.
ROOT	Point?
DAVID	Why you're here?
ROOT	Ah, that. Yes. Well I thought I'd come along personally, seeing I know you and your wife, and find out if you can throw any light on Mrs Beck's story.
DAVID	And what's backache Beck complaining about now? Too much volume on the telly, too much singing in the bath? She's always complaining about something or other. (DAVID *picks up the whisky bottle to refill his glass and is puzzled as to where the glass has gone. It is not where he left it. Baffled.*) Strange . . . (*He finds a fresh glass and fills that instead.*)
ROOT	Actually it was more of a report than a complaint.
DAVID	(*Dismissing it.*) Well, whatever it was, it'll be a waste of your time.

ROOT	Oh?
DAVID	Well, the woman's a crackpot. Quite potty. She has the most sensitive ears for miles. She could put bats out of business.
ROOT	Then perhaps we should listen to her.
DAVID	I wouldn't bother.
ROOT	I'm afraid I have to in this particular instance.
DAVID	Why, what's the old bag moaning about now?
ROOT	She says she heard the sound of a shot.
DAVID	A shot?
ROOT	Two shots, actually.
DAVID	Two shots?
ROOT	Yes, between one and three. From a gun perhaps?
DAVID	A gun? But I don't possess such a thing.
ROOT	I didn't say the shots came from here.
DAVID	Then why are you here?
ROOT	Well, as it happens she did think the shots came from this flat . . .
DAVID	Aha!
ROOT	. . . but I would rather surmise direction and location of these shots if you don't mind. We are trained in these things.
DAVID	Well she's wrong, as I said I don't own a gun.

Root	Well I didn't think it likely you would own a gun and I told her that, but she insists that just before five o'clock she heard two shots.
David	(*Looks at his watch.*) Just before five eh? It's taken you a long time to react, hasn't it?
Root	We did call earlier, actually. About five-thirty. But there was no reply.
David	Over half an hour to respond to so-called 'shots'? I can see that you, too, have your doubts about Mrs Beck.
Root	No, we got down here as soon as possible. The delay was because Mrs Beck came down to the station personally.
David	Oh? Why didn't she phone?
Root	Apparently it's out of order. BT have been informed.
David	Well, anyway it's not surprising you found no one here. I was at my office in Covent Garden.
	(Root *takes notes.*)
Root	I see.
David	So these shots, if they ever existed, must have come from one of the other flats.
Root	Mrs Beck was quite adamant it was *this* flat.
David	Have you checked the others?
Root	Yes, on our last visit. Only one person was in. Old Colonel Grant in number seven on the top floor. Didn't hear a thing. Had his iPod on listening to *The Sex Pistols*.

DAVID	Well I expect it's all quite innocent. A car backfiring. Or perhaps someone opening some bubbly? I'm sure you'll find some perfectly good explanation.
ROOT	Or another witness to the shooting?
DAVID	Who said anything about a shooting, Inspector? (*Laughs.*) Now, if you'll excuse the pun, you're jumping the gun. All you said was that Mrs Beck heard the sound of shots.
ROOT	True. As well as what she believes was your wife screaming.
DAVID	(*Amused.*) WHAT?? (*Dismissing it.*) Oh for goodness sake, it could have been anything. The woman probably had her TV up too loud. No doubt watching some awful afternoon western.
ROOT	Unlikely, if her hearing is as good as you say.
DAVID	Yes, well this really is a waste of police resources.
ROOT	Perhaps, but we have to investigate all reports. No matter how far-fetched some of them might appear to be.
DAVID	I suppose so.
ROOT	In fact this isn't the first time. Mrs Beck says she's heard things before.
DAVID	Like what?
ROOT	Like you and your wife having noisy rows. Screaming blue murder at each other.
DAVID	Well that's not a crime, is it?

(*A pause.* ROOT *stares at* DAVID.)

ROOT: Incidentally, where is your wife at the moment?

DAVID: Er . . . at the studios, I suppose.

(ROOT *checks something in his notebook.*)

ROOT: Yes, that's what I thought, but the funny thing is she left the studios more than two hours ago.

DAVID: Did she? How do you know that?

ROOT: When I got back to the station, I rang them. After all, shots were heard coming from this flat and Sarah Seeton is a famous actress.

DAVID: How very thorough of you.

ROOT: All part of the job. Any idea when she'll be home?

DAVID: I haven't the foggiest, Inspector. My wife is a law unto herself. She could be anywhere.

ROOT: The studio told me she left with your brother Robert, (*Checks his notebook.*), at three-thirty.

DAVID: Maybe she's still with him? Have you contacted him?

ROOT: No. He's not at his home.

DAVID: I'm sure he'll turn up eventually.

ROOT: I thought he might be here.

DAVID: *Here?* Why on earth would he be here?

(ROOT *notes* DAVID's *abrupt reaction.*)

ROOT: Well he is your brother . . .

DAVID	We're not joined at the hip, you know!
ROOT	And besides, I thought he'd be bringing your wife back. I believe he gave her a lift this morning.
DAVID	(*Much relieved.*) I see. Yes, yes he did.
ROOT	I wonder where they have been for the last few hours?
DAVID	No idea.
ROOT	Of course, if they did come back here, you wouldn't know anyway would you? Being in the West End all afternoon.
DAVID	That's right.
	(*A moment of silence as* ROOT *thinks.*)
ROOT	What time did you leave your office?
DAVID	Er . . . let's see, just after five, I think.
ROOT	And how did you travel?
DAVID	By cab.
ROOT	Arriving home at . . . what?
DAVID	Oh, I don't know, ten to six, five to six. The traffic was appalling. Look, what is this? You're cross-examining me like I'm in the dock of the Old Bailey.
ROOT	Just asking some simple questions.
DAVID	Yes, well I think I've answered enough of them. No matter how long it took me to get home there is absolutely no way I could have been here when . . . (*He abruptly stops.*)

ROOT	When what?
DAVID	When Mrs Beck claims she heard these so-called . . . shots.
ROOT	We may soon have conclusive evidence about that fact.
DAVID	Well even if you do, even if the whole of South Ken heard these famous 'shots', what does it prove?
ROOT	It proves Mrs Beck was not mistaken with her hearing, for one thing.
DAVID	Oh goody, goody. Three cheers for Mrs Beck and her bat-like ears!
	(*A pause.* ROOT *looks at* DAVID *closely.*)
ROOT	I hope you'll excuse me for asking this but you haven't done anything to your wife, have you, Mr Woods?
DAVID	I beg your pardon?
ROOT	Well, gunshots are heard. Anything could have happened.
DAVID	For goodness sake, she just hasn't come home yet.
ROOT	I have to ask, what with the history of domestic rows . . .
DAVID	Everyone has rows.
ROOT	You could have had a fight. Maybe things got unintentionally out of control? An accident might have happened.

DAVID	For heaven's sake Inspector, nothing's happened!
ROOT	Would you have any objection if I took a look around? Just to satisfy myself.
DAVID	Be my guest. (*He mixes himself a drink and clinks the ice cubes around his glass.*)
	(ROOT *goes through the archway. A moment's pause and then he returns.*)
DAVID	No bodies in the bathroom, Inspector? No blood on the duvet?
	(ROOT *goes into the kitchen. Nothing unusual. He is about to come back when he suddenly notices the dumb-waiter door. To* DAVID'S *horror,* ROOT *walks towards it.* DAVID *quickly follows him.* ROOT *starts to open the dumb-waiter door when the front door opens and* SARAH *walks in. She is dressed as the last time we saw her and wearing her big hat. She is carrying* ROBERT'S *case.* DAVID *stares at her in total confusion and gasps.*)
SARAH	(*Surprised at seeing* DAVID.) David?
	(*Hearing* SARAH *causes* ROOT *to turn around thereby putting his back to the dumb-waiter as he slides the door open.* ROBERT'S *corpse can be clearly seen by the audience and* DAVID. ROOT *then slides the door shut and comes straight back into the lounge, having not seen the corpse.*)
SARAH	(*Sees* ROOT.) Inspector . . . er Herb? (*She puts* ROBERT'S *case down.*)
ROOT	Root! Good evening Miss Seeton, nice to see you again.

SARAH	What on earth are you doing here?
ROOT	I was just asking your husband some questions.
SARAH	Oh?
ROOT	Yes, I had a report of two shots being heard coming from this flat.
SARAH	Two shots? How intriguing.
ROOT	Mrs Beck downstairs. Swears she heard them just before five o'clock.
SARAH	(*Not taking it at all seriously.*) The only shots you'd come across about five in this flat would be my afternoon gin and tonic which at, (*Looks at her watch*), nearly six-thirty is well overdue. Would you mind, darling?
	(*A totally stunned* DAVID *goes to the drinks cabinet and mixes her drink.*)
SARAH	Why not join me for one, Inspector?
ROOT	Er . . . no, thanks all the same. Time I was making tracks.
SARAH	As you wish. Anyway, I'm sure you'll find Mrs Beck imagined it all. She watches far too much television.
ROOT	Yes, well you're both probably right. I'd better check with my colleague and get back to the station. This has taken enough time.
	(DAVID *hands the drink to* SARAH.)
DAVID	(*To* ROOT.) I tried to tell you that before. Perhaps you won't pay quite so much heed to a babbling old bag, with above average hearing, who fancies herself as Miss Marple.

Root	(*Slightly embarrassed.*) Yes, well good evening then.
Sarah	Cheerio, Inspector.
	(Root *exits through the front door.*
	David *faces* Sarah *in total silence not sure what to say or how to play it.* Sarah *slams her drink down.*)
Sarah	OH MY GOD, DAVID!!
David	What . . . What on earth's the matter?
Sarah	(*Catching her breath.*) Something terrible has happened. Something's . . .
David	What?
Sarah	(*Trying to compose herself.*) I've done something . . . I . . . I . . . don't know where to start.
David	For heaven's sake pull yourself together! Calm down and start at the beginning. Now, what's happened?
Sarah	Your . . . Your brother's dead.
David	DEAD???
Sarah	I killed him.
David	WHAT??
Sarah	I killed him. Look . . .
	(*She walks over to the dumb-waiter and slides the door back.* Robert's *corpse is still in there. Half of him falls out of the compartment. His open eyes stare out.*)

DAVID	(*Pretending to be horrified.*) WHAT!! For goodness sake, Sarah! Are you sure he's dead?
	(DAVID *holds* ROBERT'S *wrist as he goes through the motions of feeling his pulse.*)
SARAH	Of course I'm sure! Look at him! He's not grabbing forty winks is he? He's dead. I killed him in the basement car park.
DAVID	What the hell happened??
SARAH	(*Taking a deep breath.*) We came back here to do some rehearsing and we used some prop guns from the studio . . .
DAVID	Prop guns??
SARAH	Well, I don't understand how but they were loaded and I . . . I . . .
DAVID	Shot him?
SARAH	No! No, well . . . yes but I thought the gun was empty. Look . . .
	(*She takes one of the guns out of* ROBERT'S *case and waves it around as she explains what happened.* DAVID *is horrified and tries to grab it off her.*)
DAVID	BE CAREFUL!!
SARAH	(*Wildly waving the gun.*) It went bang and he fell with blood streaming down his face but . . . but he was only faking . . . Look, your brother tried to kill me, David! He was going to shoot me. He had the gun at my head.
	(*With great relief,* DAVID *finally gets hold of the gun.*)

DAVID	But Robert? Why would Robert do that?
SARAH	I DON'T KNOW!! It was something to do with his wig.
DAVID	His wig??
SARAH	He was convinced that I'd told the press about it.
DAVID	For goodness sake!
SARAH	Anyway, never mind that. The next thing I know I'm backing away from him. It just mysteriously went off by itself . . .
DAVID	His wig?
SARAH	NO! HIS GUN!
DAVID	So Mrs Beck did hear two shots. Did he hit you?
SARAH	No, the bullet missed but then he attacked me. He smashed me against the table and knocked me out. (*She points to her head.*)
DAVID	Show me.
	(*She takes her hat off.* DAVID *inspects the back of her head.*)
	You'd better see a doctor.
SARAH	NO!
DAVID	Why not?
SARAH	For the same reason that I didn't tell that Inspector. I've committed murder, for heaven's sake! I've killed your brother.
	(DAVID *stares at her in total horror.*)

SARAH	When I came round Robert was dragging me along the ground in the basement car park. But I broke free. He produced his gun and was going to use it but I . . . I . . . just grabbed it and in the struggle it went off . . . again. Whoever makes those guns should be shot.
DAVID	I don't believe it. Prop guns? Bullets? Wigs? What the devil were the two of you playing at?
SARAH	(*Almost hysterical.*) IT WAS EITHER HIM OR ME, DAVID!! Then I panicked. I couldn't decide what to do with his body. If I left it there, one of the other flat owners may have seen it.
DAVID	So what did you do?
SARAH	I didn't know what to do. In the end I dragged his body over to the dumb-waiter and hauled him up.
DAVID	Okay, okay. That's probably the best thing you could have done.
SARAH	My mind was all over the place. I eventually pulled myself together and decided to come up when I saw the police car outside. I didn't know what to do so I waited and waited . . . In the end I just *had* to come up.
DAVID	You did right.
SARAH	I thought they might be visiting another flat. I nearly died when I saw that bloody Inspector. I was so scared.
DAVID	Well you didn't show it. You gave a remarkable performance. For once.
SARAH	What are you? A critic?
DAVID	Where's the other gun?

SARAH	(*Points at* ROBERT'S *case.*) In his case.
DAVID	We'll dump them somewhere. What we have to decide now, though, is what to do with his body.
SARAH	Perhaps if I just went to the police and told them the whole thing exactly as it happened.
DAVID	NO!!!
	(SARAH *reacts.*)
	What I mean is I don't think they'll believe a word of it. And a jury certainly wouldn't and even if they did, think what it will do to your public image. You'll never work again.
SARAH	But surely after I explain . . .
DAVID	We can't take the risk, Sarah. We must get rid of his body.
SARAH	I don't know . . . I can't even think straight.
DAVID	Leave that to me. We're still a team, even in these dreadful circumstances.
SARAH	Thank God I've got you to help me.
	(*She grips his hand when something suddenly strikes her.*)
SARAH	But . . . But how come you came home? I'd arranged to meet you at your office.
DAVID	(*Unsure of his reply.*) I . . . I . . . left some client's files behind. I had to get them. He's got a tax hearing on Friday.
SARAH	I see.

DAVID	We must act quickly. Where did Robert park his car?
SARAH	His car? It's . . . down the street. Near the square. (*She pours herself a stiff drink.*)
	(DAVID *searches* ROBERT'S *pockets. He first finds the pink fluffy keyring which he quickly pockets without* SARAH *seeing. He then finds* ROBERT'S *car keys.*)
DAVID	Right, I'll drive it. We'll put his body in the boot of your car and you follow me. We'll go out into the country, find some disused lane and leave him in his own car for the police to find.
SARAH	There must be some other way . . .
DAVID	SARAH, I'M NOT GOING TO FILL THE BATH WITH ACID!!
	(*Suddenly* ROBERT'S *arm falls out of the dumb-waiter.* SARAH *screams.*)
DAVID	Pull yourself together!! I'll go and change into some old clothes. (*He exits through the archway.*)
	(SARAH *looks around the room for her car keys. She can't see them.*)
SARAH	Where are my car keys?
DAVID	(*Off.*) I don't know . . . wherever you left them.
	(SARAH *goes over to the desk and looks on top of it for the car keys. She can't find them so she decides to look in the desk drawer. Inside she finds the typed manuscript and takes it out to search underneath it. The title page catches her eye. She quietly reads it out loud.*)

SARAH	(*Baffled.*) "Soap plus Scandal plus Sex add up to Sarah Seeton"???
	(*She flicks through some pages. She can't believe what she sees. Her face turns to horror as she rapidly scans one page after another. DAVID is about to enter through the archway when he sees her. He quickly retreats back into the hallway. She doesn't see him.*)
DAVID	(*Off.*) Found them?
	(*She hurriedly returns the manuscript into the drawer and closes it.*)
	DAVID *now comes back into the room. He's wearing an old anorak. He pulls on some gloves.*)
DAVID	Got them?
SARAH	(*Searching on top of desk.*) Er . . . No.
DAVID	I'm sure I . . . (*Without her noticing he takes the pink fluffy keyring out of his pocket and places it on the mantelpiece.*) Here they are.
	(*He picks them up and hands them to her.*)
SARAH	I thought I'd looked there.
DAVID	Give me a hand with the body.
	(DAVID *walks into the kitchen, followed by* SARAH. *Then, between them they manage to stuff* ROBERT'S *corpse back into the dumb-waiter compartment.* DAVID *slides the door shut and is about to start pulling the rope when* SARAH *speaks.*)
SARAH	Why . . . Why don't I go down there first?

DAVID	Why?
SARAH	Make sure that Inspector's gone.
DAVID	He's bound to have gone by now.
SARAH	(*Insistent.*) We can't take the risk. I'll go down and shout up the shaft that it's all clear. Then you pull the rope, lower him down and *then* join me.

(DAVID *stares at her, unconvinced.*)

SARAH	Just in case. It's better to be on the safe side.
DAVID	All right, if you insist . . .

(*They come back into the lounge. He looks at her, she looks at him. There is an uncertain moment and* SARAH *makes a dash for the front door.* DAVID *runs across the room, gets there first and blocks her way. They wrestle a little.*)

SARAH	Get out of my way, David.
DAVID	I daresay you're wondering about that manuscript.
SARAH	GET OUT OF MY WAY!!
DAVID	I can explain.
SARAH	Let me past!

(*He pulls the gun out of his anorak pocket. She slowly backs away from him.*)

SARAH	What are you doing??
DAVID	I really didn't want to have to do this.
SARAH	Have you gone mad? Put the bloody gun away!

DAVID	No.
SARAH	Put the gun down, David.
DAVID	(*Shouts.*) NO! SIT DOWN!
	(SARAH *sits down.* DAVID *walks over to the desk and takes the manuscript out of the drawer. He gives it to* SARAH.)
DAVID	Go on. Have a look. It's your biggest role ever. Featured on every page.
SARAH	(*Playing for time.*) This is what you were writing in Paris?
DAVID	Yep. Thought I'd try a biography for a change. Night and day I typed. Blank sheets, messy ribbons, aching wrists . . .
	(*A pause as* SARAH *sees the light.*)
SARAH	It was *you*. You arranged for Robert to kill me, didn't you?
DAVID	We've been building up to this for months.
	(SARAH *looks horrified.*)
DAVID	The plan was to put *your* body in the boot of your car and leave you somewhere where the police would eventually find you.
SARAH	And with me dead you two would have a bestseller on your hands. Is that it?
DAVID	Ten out of ten! Go to the top of the class, that girl.
SARAH	(*Throws the manuscript on the floor.*) Bastard!

DAVID	Believe me, I didn't want to do this, Sarah. (*He aims the gun directly at her.*)
SARAH	(*Stands up.*) THEN FOR GOD'S SAKE DON'T!!! (*She backs away from him.*)
DAVID	I have no choice . . .
SARAH	Remember one thing, David, as soon as you pull that trigger you're a killer. You'll have two bodies to dispose of. If things go wrong, you could spend the rest of your life in prison. You wouldn't like that, David. Funny things happening in the showers.
DAVID	What . . . What could go wrong?
SARAH	It's your finger on the trigger. (*He starts pulling the trigger.*) *Your* finger . . .
	(*Suddenly* DAVID *releases his finger and lowers the gun. An idea has dawned on him.*)
DAVID	Not necessarily.
SARAH	What?
DAVID	Why don't I let little brother kill you?
SARAH	Robert? He's dead. How can a dead man kill me?
DAVID	In a way he's already done it. (*He picks up the video camera off the desk and flips open the viewing screen.*) You see I have a wonderful recording of him shooting you and vice-versa. Pity to let it go to waste.
	(SARAH *stares at the video camera.*)

SARAH	You've done what? You filmed us as well as writing a book? What were you going to do? Put it on *You've Been Framed*??
DAVID	It'll make a perfect alibi. I'll tell the police that we were all messing around with the video camera, doing the old home movies bit when things went wrong. Tragically wrong. The guns were mistakenly loaded with real bullets and you were both killed. Two dead bodies and the whole thing neatly recorded for posterity by one totally horrified and innocent cameraman. Moi.
SARAH	No-one will believe you.
DAVID	Why ever not? The proof will be there for all to see.
SARAH	(*Inspired.*) It won't work, there's only one gunshot.
	(DAVID *shakes his head at her mistake.*)
DAVID	Wrong! The sound didn't come out. (*Like a whining technophobe.*) "I was always hopeless with gadgets, Inspector . . ."
SARAH	But he's been dead for two hours.
DAVID	Stuck in that freezing cold dumb-waiter? By the time the ambulance gets here, he'll be back to room temperature. It'll look like you both died at the same time.
	(SARAH *has surreptitiously dipped her hand into* ROBERT's *case and brought out the other gun. She points it at* DAVID.)
SARAH	Put down the gun, David.
DAVID	Don't be silly.

SARAH	Put it down darling. I'll have no hesitation in using this.
DAVID	But that's the gun you fired the blank with. It's got no bullets in it.
SARAH	How do you know? The guns are identical. I just pulled the one I gave you out of the case at random.
DAVID	Yes, but I checked it just now in the bedroom. Two bullets left.

(SARAH *pulls the trigger on her gun. To her horror it clicks.*)

SARAH	(*Almost in tears.*) You're crazy!
DAVID	AND YOU, MY DARLING, ARE DEAD!!

(DAVID *swiftly aims his gun at* SARAH'S *heart and fires. There's a loud crack of a gunshot and she collapses in front of the fireplace, dead.*)

DAVID	Let's hope you heard that one, Mrs Beck. And this one too.

(*He fires another shot into the wall and walks over to dig the bullet out. He pockets it. He crosses to the telephone and calmly dials 999. He injects a sense of real panic into his voice.*)

(*On the phone.*) Ambulance please . . . Hello? I need an ambulance as soon as you can . . . Right, David Woods . . . number three, Ffoulkes Mansions, Ffoulkes Gardens . . . It's double "F"s actually . . . SW7 . . . Of course it's an emergency. There's been a terrible accident, a shooting, my wife and my brother . . . Please hurry!

(*He replaces the phone. He then drags* ROBERT'S *corpse over to the fireplace where he places it alongside* SARAH'S *dead body. Watching the frozen frame on the video camera viewing screen, (which the audience cannot see), he then carefully arranges the bodies of* SARAH *and* ROBERT *into exactly the same position they are on the screen. Satisfied he has positioned them just right, he places his gun in* ROBERT'S *right hand, curling his index finger around the trigger.* SARAH, *of course, is still holding the other gun. He remembers their hats and puts them on their heads.*)

DAVID Now I just wipe the rest of the film . . . (*He operates a button on the video camera.*) That's all folks! Just freeze that action for me a little while longer.

(*He suddenly sees the manuscript on the floor and picks it up.*)

Damn! I'll have to rewrite the final chapter.

(*An emergency siren can be heard in the distance.*

Blackout.)

Scene Two.

Nine months later, late afternoon. The room is much as before but all the personal photographs and awards have been taken down and there are dust sheets over some of the furniture. Some brand new hardback copies of DAVID'S *book about* SARAH *are piled up on the desk.* DAVID, *wearing bright holiday clothes, enters through the archway struggling with two large suitcases. He puts them down when the front door bell rings. He opens the door to find* MRS BECK *standing there. She's wearing bright lipstick and appears a little tipsy.*

DAVID	Oh it's you. What do you want?
MRS BECK	(*All charm and smiles.*) I just thought I'd pop up and wish you bon voyage, Mr Woods. (*She enters.*)
DAVID	I'll be back in three weeks.
MRS BECK	Australia, isn't it?
DAVID	Not that it's any of your business, but yes. They're hoping to repeat the success of my book over there. The advance orders are big plus big equals ginormous.

(MRS BECK *wanders over to the desk and picks up a copy of* DAVID'S *book about* SARAH. *It has a photograph of* SARAH *on its cover.*)

MRS BECK	I always said you'd write a bestseller.
DAVID	Have you been drinking?
MRS BECK	Oh, don't mind if I do. (*She helps herself to a bottle of gin off the drinks cabinet and looks for a glass to pour it into.*) Where are all your glasses?
DAVID	I don't know. Lately they all seem to have mysteriously disappeared.

(MRS BECK *produces a glass from one of her pouches.* DAVID *gives her an odd look as he half-recognises his property.*)

MRS BECK	Just as well I've got one here then. (*She fills the glass with gin.*) I knew you had talent. Didn't I always say you had talent?
DAVID	Not that I can recall. (*He throws a dust sheet over a chair.*)

MRS BECK	My friends are so impressed what with me being mentioned in the book three times. A right little celebrity I am down at the 'Dog and Garter'.
DAVID	Yes, well you were part of the general scenario. Busybodying about when you thought you heard shots.
MRS BECK	I did hear shots.
DAVID	The second time, yes. The first time you were obviously mistaken.
MRS BECK	I still reckon I heard something. Anyway, there I am in a bestseller. Pity you spelt my name wrong, though. Calling me Mrs Back.
DAVID	Printer's error, Mrs Beck. I'll see they correct it in the cheap paperback edition. Now if you don't mind, I'm expecting my taxi at any minute.
MRS BECK	Well don't you worry. I'll keep an eye on this place while you're away.
DAVID	That won't be necessary.
MRS BECK	And then maybe when you get back, we could have one of my fish suppers together?
DAVID	I don't think so. I've never been much of a fishy type.
MRS BECK	You wait till you taste my smoked kipper.
	(*The intercom buzzes.*)
DAVID	That'll be my cab. (*He walks over to the intercom and speaks into it.*) Can you come up? I've got some cases and things. (*He presses the buzzer.*)

MRS BECK	Right, well I'll be off then. Have a good trip.
	(*She's about to leave when she rushes over to him and plants a smacker of a kiss on the side of his face. Then she exits.*)
DAVID	Yuck!! (*He wipes away the lipstick with a handkerchief.*)
	(DAVID *then goes through the archway and returns with an airline bag. He starts to pack his books into it. The front doorbell rings.* DAVID *opens the door and finds* ROOT *standing there.* ROOT *is wearing a navy blue sailor's cap and is carrying a large brown envelope.*)
DAVID	The cases are just here . . . (*Surprised.*) Inspector?
ROOT	Good afternoon, Mr Woods. Trust I'm not disturbing you.
DAVID	I'm sorry, I thought you were my cab driver. What on earth are you doing here? I haven't seen you for ages.
ROOT	About eight months, actually. The day of the inquest.
DAVID	Oh yes. Well, what do you want? I'm just about to leave for the airport.
	(ROOT *enters.*)
ROOT	Ah, well I'm glad I've caught you then.
DAVID	Caught me?
ROOT	Well you're just off somewhere and I'm about to set sail myself in the morning. We could have easily missed each other.

DAVID	Oh?
ROOT	Yes, I've finally bought that motor cruiser I always fancied. I thought I'd kick off my retirement with a bit of sailing. I'm leaving for Jersey first thing in the morning provided the weather holds.
DAVID	You're retired?
ROOT	Will be tomorrow. This is my final day on the job.
DAVID	Really? Well the best of luck, Inspector, I'm sure it's well-deserved. But what is it you want to see me about?
ROOT	Oh yes, I was in my local bookshop yesterday buying some reading material for the voyage and I happened to come across a huge display for your book. Very impressive.
DAVID	The old hard sell, I'm afraid. My publishers are pushing like mad to make it the number one Christmas bestseller. It's well on the way incidentally, straight in at number three.
ROOT	Well they certainly persuaded me. (*He takes a copy of* DAVID's *book out of his envelope.*) I couldn't resist buying a copy. And then I thought, I wonder if Mr Woods *would* sign it for me? (*He titters.*) Just a little joke of mine.
DAVID	Well . . .
ROOT	That's if it's not too much trouble.
DAVID	(*Takes his book.*) No, of course it isn't. (*He searches his pockets looking in vain for a pen.*)
ROOT	Hang on . . . (*He offers him a ballpoint.*)
DAVID	Thanks. Now what shall I write?

ROOT	Um . . . Would you mind putting "To Tyrone Root, with regards and best wishes . . ." Something like that?
DAVID	Not at all. (*Chuckles.*) Tyrone . . .
	(DAVID *takes the book over to the desk and starts to write the inscription.*)
DAVID	Oh! It's run out of ink. (*Lightly.*) Wouldn't be much good if you had to take "notes" would it?
ROOT	(*Laughs.*) Any "notes" today will be confined to the old memory.
DAVID	I'll get another one. (*He exits through the archway.*)
	(*As soon as he's gone,* ROOT *walks around the room, sizing angles up and mentally measuring distances. He's obviously onto something but we get the feeling that even he isn't quite sure what, yet.*
	DAVID *returns through the archway holding a fountain pen.*)
DAVID	Found one. (*He goes over to the desk and writes the inscription.*)
ROOT	You know, I've been very rude.
DAVID	Oh?
ROOT	There was I waffling on about my retirement and my boat and everything and I never asked where you were going.
DAVID	Sydney, actually.
ROOT	Sydney?

DAVID	Yes, for the Australian launch of my book. There's a lot of interest. Sarah's TV show is a big hit down under. Our revenge for *Neighbours*.
ROOT	I can imagine.
DAVID	(*Handing him the book.*) Be sure to let the ink dry for a moment.
ROOT	Thank you. (*He blows on the ink.*) I've already read bits of this in my paper, you know.
DAVID	Serialisation, I'm afraid. Name of the game in publishing now. One writes a personal story about someone, something private and tender, and it goes in one end of the machine and gets spewed out the other. Syndication, serialisation, documentaries, chat shows . . . The list's endless. I had no idea when I put my thoughts down on paper just what was ahead of me.
ROOT	No, I'm sure you didn't.
DAVID	But if I hadn't written it, someone else would have done. At least my version is as near to the truth as could possibly be.
ROOT	Quite. The bit about how your wife died must have been particularly distressing to write.
DAVID	Yes, it was.
ROOT	A most unfortunate accident.
DAVID	Well, if you remember, that's exactly how the Coroner's Court described it. Accidental death. (*Hopelessly.*) There was nothing I could do. I just watched the whole thing through the eyepiece.
ROOT	Dreadful.

(DAVID *starts packing his books into the airline bag.*)

DAVID At first I thought they were just play-acting but then I realised . . .

ROOT Strange how your brother told you they were prop guns when in actual fact they were real ones, wasn't it?

DAVID Not really. As I said at the Inquest, I believe he planned the whole thing. As you know, he was very depressed about being written out of the show. Poor Robert.

ROOT But why would he want to shoot your wife as well?

DAVID As I said in my book, he was one of her many lovers.

ROOT Even less reason then.

DAVID Who knows, Inspector? Maybe Sarah had decided to end the affair and he couldn't handle it. Could have been any number of reasons but one thing's for certain, we'll never know now.

ROOT No, I suppose we won't.

DAVID Anyway, if you don't mind I'd rather not relive that terrible evening again.

ROOT No, of course not. (*Pointedly.*) It's all in your book, anyway. Very detailed.

DAVID Yes. Now, if you wouldn't mind, my taxi will be here any second and . . .

ROOT (*Closing his book up.*) Right, well thanks for signing this. It's been a pleasure to see you again. I hope all goes well in Sydney.

DAVID	Thank you, and I hope you enjoy your nautical retirement, Inspector.
ROOT	I'm sure I shall. Goodbye, Mr Woods.
	(*They shake hands and* ROOT *opens the front door to leave when he suddenly remembers something.*)
ROOT	Oh, I nearly forgot, there was just one other thing.
DAVID	(*Fed up.*) Your middle name is Columbo? . . .
ROOT	Trust it to happen on my last day but there you go. This morning a South African woman was arrested at Heathrow airport. Diamond smuggler.
DAVID	(*After a pause.*) Oh? And what does that have to do with me?
ROOT	The woman's name is Hannah Van Lee. Have you ever heard of her?
DAVID	Van Lee? No, I don't think so.
ROOT	Comes from a town called Umzimvubu.
DAVID	Umzimvubu?
ROOT	Umzimvubu. It's near Durban.
DAVID	Never heard of it. Or her.
ROOT	Perhaps this picture might jog your memory.
	(*He takes a photo of* HANNAH *out of the brown envelope and hands it to* DAVID.)
DAVID	(*Looking at the photo.*) No, I'm quite sure that I . . .

Root	Think carefully, because I have some information . . .
David	No, I'm positive I've never seen her before.
Root	You're quite certain?
David	Yes. (*He looks at the photograph again.*) Quite certain.
Root	So what would you say if I told you that she claims to have met *you*?
David	In Umzimvubu?
Root	No, in this flat.

(*A deafening silence.* David *isn't quite sure what to say.*)

David	Well she's obviously mistaken.
Root	She's naming names, hoping to get a lighter sentence. Yours came up.
David	How absurd. I've never heard of her.
Root	Now I know this is going to sound utterly ridiculous but she says that you invited her into this flat and in exchange for the return of diamonds that you stole from her . . .
David	WHAT??
Root	. . . you asked her to film the murder of your wife.
David	MURDER!! She must be bonkers!
Root	Well, in all fairness, she's given me a fairly detailed plan of this flat.
David	Really?

ROOT	Yes.
DAVID	(*Inspired.*) Oh that's easily explained.
ROOT	Is it?
DAVID	Yes, about two years ago Sarah did a feature for one of the glossy magazines. You know, one of those 'at home with the stars' things. She must have seen it.
ROOT	Perhaps. But she did seem pretty convincing, all the same.
DAVID	Surely you don't believe her? You know only too well how Sarah died. And my brother Robert. I was here. I filmed it. The idea of murder is insane.
ROOT	I know only too well of *your* account of how they died.
DAVID	How else could it have happened? A South African from Umzimvubu? Stolen diamonds? Detailed plans of this flat? The whole thing is preposterous.
ROOT	Yes. I expect you're right but if I want to kick her story out on its ear, which I suspect is where it belongs, I've got to satisfy myself with your story, haven't I?
DAVID	I gave you my "story", as you put it, at the time.
ROOT	Let's just go through it one more time shall we? For my benefit.
DAVID	Inspector, I don't wish to be uncooperative but I have a plane to catch. My taxi will be here any minute.

ROOT	Well it's not here yet is it? This won't take long. Let's start with your video camera.
DAVID	My video camera?
ROOT	Yes, the one you were using when your wife was killed.
DAVID	But I've packed it.
	(ROOT *says nothing.* DAVID *reluctantly unzips one of his cases and brings out the video camera, which he then hands to* ROOT.)
ROOT	Now, you claim you were standing . . . where?
DAVID	Oh, I don't know . . . about here I suppose. (*He takes any position facing the fireplace as long as it's not near the wooden chest.*)
ROOT	Are you sure?
DAVID	As sure as I can be. It's not something I've tried to remember.
	(ROOT *stands behind him and looks through the camera eyepiece.*)
ROOT	Hmm, it's as I thought.
DAVID	What is?
ROOT	I'm not happy, not happy at all. Since Hannah Van Lee's accusation against you, I've dug out the original video recording you made and had a close look at it. And something that struck me straight away was the angle of the shot.
DAVID	The angle of the shot?
ROOT	Yes, let me show you.

	(*He hands* DAVID *the video camera and takes a photo out of his envelope.*)
ROOT	This is a print from your recording. If you look carefully you can see that fireplace, (*Points at the fireplace.*), in the background.
DAVID	(*Looking at the photo.*) So?
ROOT	Why don't you move around the room until what you see through the eyepiece corresponds to what is in the photograph. That is until you can see the fireplace.
DAVID	Is this really necessary?
ROOT	Please. If you wouldn't mind.
	(*Glancing from time to time at the photograph that* ROOT *is holding, a fed-up* DAVID, *looking through the eyepiece, moves around the room. He offers one position to* ROOT *who looks through the eyepiece, checks his photograph and then shakes his head.* DAVID *then moves to another position and again suggests the position to* ROOT.)
ROOT	(*Looking through the eyepiece and then checking the photograph again.*) No, no . . .
	(DAVID *is now standing directly in front of the wooden chest.*)
DAVID	About here I suppose.
ROOT	Let's have a look.
	(ROOT *comes up behind him and squints through the eyepiece over* DAVID's *shoulder.*)
ROOT	No, still not the right angle. Perhaps if you were a bit lower?

	(DAVID *crouches a little.* ROOT *looks through the eyepiece again.*)
ROOT	A little bit more?
	(DAVID *is now on his knees in front of the wooden chest.*)
DAVID	This is absurd.
ROOT	(*Taking the camera and looking through the eyepiece.*) That's it. If you'd been in this position you would have filmed the fireplace. Especially if you'd been hiding inside this chest. (*He taps the chest.*)
DAVID	(*Mock surprise.*) *Inside* the chest?
ROOT	Yes. That's where Hannah Van Lee claims she was when your brother killed your wife. Didn't I mention it?
DAVID	No you did not! (*Standing up straight again.*) In the chest indeed? Her story gets more outrageous by the minute.
ROOT	She says she filmed through the gap. Just before five o'clock.
DAVID	Well perhaps I was standing over here, I can't remember, but you can dismiss her crackpot story immediately. You saw my wife with your own eyes at six-thirty. So how could she have been killed before five? It doesn't make sense.
ROOT	Yes but looking through the case history again, I was intrigued by that call from Mrs Beck downstairs.
DAVID	We're all intrigued by things that woman does.

ROOT   If you remember, she told us that just before five she heard a shot as well as someone who sounded like your wife screaming.

DAVID   But for pity's sake, Inspector, she was obviously wrong when my wife, in excellent health witnessed by your good self, walked through that door an hour and a half later.

ROOT   That's correct. I left just after.

DAVID   And very shortly after that, after Robert got here, was the accident with the guns. The accident that I saw and filmed with that very video camera.

ROOT   Just after seven?

DAVID   That's right. I'm sure the log of my 999 call confirmed that.

ROOT   Yes. The thing is I'm still not totally convinced *you* made that film. Hannah Van Lee's wild story certainly seems to tie in with what Mrs Beck heard, doesn't it?

DAVID   (*Hammering the point home.*) BUT YOU SAW MY WIFE WITH YOUR OWN EYES AT SIX-THIRTY.

ROOT   Yes, so you keep saying.

DAVID   And I'll keep saying it. Because it's what happened. It's the truth.

ROOT   According to Hannah Van Lee, the truth is that you and your brother conspired to murder your wife.

DAVID   (*Exploding.*) WHAT!!

ROOT	She claims you told her that the two of you planned this book, (*He holds up his copy of the book.*) months before the accident. But the only reason it would be a bestseller was if your wife was dead. The death your brother agreed to carry out whilst you were safely at work. But then you got greedy, didn't you? You decided to have the murder filmed so you could blackmail your brother into giving up his share of the profits. And that's where Hannah Van Lee comes in.
DAVID	This is ridiculous. All right, all right if what you say is true, how come the recording shows my wife holding a gun? Rather an oversight in a well organised, premeditated murder wouldn't you say? Handing the intended victim a deadly weapon?
ROOT	Yes but it wasn't a deadly weapon *then*, was it? It was loaded with a blank. Your brother had the gun with the real bullet.
DAVID	I don't believe this.
ROOT	But then something went wrong, didn't it? According to Hannah Van Lee, Sarah wasn't shot but struck on the head and fell down. Now, let's suppose she wasn't dead but just knocked out and then later recovering, she shoots your brother. Then after I've gone, she discovers the manuscript of your book.
DAVID	My book?
ROOT	I gather the manuscript was finished and ready to be sent to publishers the day she died.
DAVID	You're talking absolute rubbish, Inspector. That book took months to write. Months of aching sheets, blank ribbons, messy wrists . . . I mean . . .

ROOT   You would have then had no option but to kill Sarah yourself. Then with two dead bodies on your hands you did the only thing left open to you and made out what happened on the video recording was for real. That they both accidentally killed each other, giving you the perfect alibi as you claimed you'd been operating the camera. It was clever, I'll give you that.

(*A pause.* DAVID *tries to keep composed.*)

DAVID   What an extraordinary imagination. All stemming from some hysterical South African from Umzim-bloody-vubu!

ROOT   You have to admit it does seem to click into place, Mr Woods.

DAVID   Even if I thought it did, you don't have a shred of evidence. You can't prove anything.

(*He grabs the video camera off* ROOT *and puts it in one of his cases, zipping it closed.*)

ROOT   Is that an admission of guilt?

DAVID   No. It's a statement of fact. (*He goes to the window and looks down into the street.*) Where's that bloody cab?

ROOT   You see it's all down to the only piece of evidence we have, the video recording. I looked at that film again and again and then I noticed something. If you look carefully enough you could see that window, (*Points at the window.*), in the background. And the curtains weren't drawn.

DAVID   (*Incredulous.*) You're not going to say that the accident could not have happened at seven o'clock because I hadn't drawn my curtains

	and therefore it must have happened earlier? (*Laughs.*) That is right out of Sherlock Holmes, Inspector.
ROOT	No, what was interesting to me was not even in this flat. It was *outside* it.
DAVID	Outside? Now you've really lost me.
	(ROOT *goes over to the window, pulls back the net curtain and looks out.*)
ROOT	That street lamp. On the video you can't see its light.
DAVID	So?
ROOT	Lighting-up time on that day was five thirty-one pm. I've checked.
	(DAVID *freezes.*)
	If you made that video as you claim just after seven, the light from that street-lamp would be quite visible. It's not. So the recording must have been made prior to five thirty-one. Say just before five, perhaps?
DAVID	Maybe the street light was faulty?
ROOT	Possibly. But it got me thinking. (*He walks over to the fireplace.*) Looking at the film again, I then noticed your clock in the background.
	(DAVID *smiles at* ROOT'S *obvious mistake.*)
DAVID	I don't think so. That clock has always been exactly there. (*Pointing at the wall clock.*) The accident took place over *there*. (*Pointing at the fireplace area on the other side of the lounge.*)

ROOT	Yes, but it was reflected in the mirror *here*. (*He points at the mirror above the fireplace.*)
	(DAVID *looks at the mirror. His mind racing to get ahead of* ROOT'*s.*)
ROOT	Unfortunately it was difficult to see what the time was on its face.
DAVID	(*Relieved.*) Focus not quite sharp enough? Oh dear, what a shame.
ROOT	So I had that part of the film blown up.
DAVID	Blown up?
ROOT	Yes.
	(ROOT *takes a large photograph out of the brown envelope. It shows a blow-up of the clock face. It's fuzzy but just possible to see that the hands read six minutes after seven o'clock. He hands the photo to* DAVID.)
ROOT	Look at this please.
DAVID	(*Examining photo.*) I hate to disappoint you, Inspector, but the hands read six minutes after seven. (*He hands the photo back.*)
ROOT	That's right. Because the video camera was filming an inverted image. But if we reflect it in the mirror . . .
	(*He holds the photo against the mirror.* DAVID *stares at the reflection in horror.*)
ROOT	The hands read six minutes before five. Which ties in precisely with Mrs Beck's hearing of two shots, the street light being off and Hannah Van Lee's account of what happened.

(D̪ᴀᴠɪᴅ *is speechless.*)

ROOT Could be pretty damning evidence couldn't it? (*He puts the photo back into the envelope.*)

DAVID Could be? What do you mean, "could be"?

ROOT What I mean is that it would be very easy for me to go back to the station and announce that Hannah Van Lee's little story didn't lead anywhere. That it was just an hysterical outburst from a desperate woman trying to avoid a prison sentence.

DAVID How much?

ROOT I beg your pardon?

DAVID How much do you want?

ROOT You're not trying to bribe me, Mr Woods, are you?

DAVID Of course I'm trying to bloody bribe you, what do you think I'm doing?

ROOT Oh good. I just wanted to be quite sure.

DAVID So how much do you want?

ROOT I'll settle for fifty thousand.

DAVID FIFTY THOUSAND POUNDS?? You must be joking.

ROOT Small price for freedom, I would have thought.

DAVID I haven't got that kind of money.

ROOT Oh come off it. You're a bestselling author. It was in the papers that you received a one

	hundred thousand pound advance for your book.
DAVID	Yes, but the money is invested. It's in shares, high interest bank accounts . . .
ROOT	All right then, forget cash. I'll take something else.
DAVID	Like what? There's nothing here worth anything like that.
ROOT	Oh there is. Your diamond ring.
	(DAVID *looks at the ring on his finger. It's the blue diamond from Act One, Scene Two.*)
DAVID	My ring? It's not worth fifty thousand pounds.
ROOT	No, according to Hannah Van Lee, it's worth a lot more.
DAVID	She told you about it?
ROOT	Yes.
DAVID	Well you're not having it.
ROOT	Oh yes I am.
DAVID	Oh no you're not.
ROOT	(*Producing a gun.*) Oh yes I am.
DAVID	(*Backing away.*) DON'T SHOOT!!
ROOT	Just give me the ring.
DAVID	All right, all right. (*He quickly tries to take the ring off his finger but can't.*) It's stuck.
ROOT	Stuck??

DAVID	It won't budge.
ROOT	Well make it budge.
DAVID	I CAN'T!
ROOT	Don't take me for an idiot. I'll shoot your bloody finger off if I have to.
DAVID	NO!! It really is stuck. Perhaps if I used a piece of soap?
ROOT	Soap??
DAVID	Or a thread of cotton? I read once in *Woman's Own* that if you get a thread of cotton and put it . . .
ROOT	I'm not farting around with threads of cotton!! Here, let me have a go . . .

(ROOT *grabs* DAVID'S *finger and starts yanking the ring off.*)

DAVID	(*In pain.*) Aaahhh!! That hurts!!
ROOT	Keep still, man!

(*He pulls the ring off* DAVID'S *finger.* DAVID *makes a grab for* ROOT'S *gun. There's a struggle. In the fracas a gunshot goes off. We don't know who's been shot and then* DAVID *slowly falls to the ground.* ROOT *watches in horror as* DAVID *dies on the floor.*

ROOT *stands motionless for a moment and then slips the ring onto his own finger. He then drags* DAVID'S *body over to the wooden chest. He opens the lid and lifts the body inside.*

The intercom buzzes. ROOT *answers it.*)

Root	(*On the intercom.*) Yes?
Voice	(*On the intercom.*) Taxi for the airport . . .
Root	(*On the intercom.*) Right. I've . . . I've changed my mind. I want to go to Chelsea Harbour. The marina. Can you bring the car up to the entrance? I've got a few things to load up . . .

(Root *closes the lid of the wooden chest. He then starts dragging it towards the front door. When he opens the door,* Mrs Beck, *dressed in waterproof sailing clothes, is standing in the doorway. He looks up at her. Suddenly the lid of the chest springs open and* David's *arm flops out.*)

Mrs Beck I told you he wouldn't fit, didn't I?

(Root *looks at her helplessly, she gives him a knowing look back.*

Mrs Beck *opens up her jacket to reveal her utility belt underneath. She selects the hack-saw from one of the pouches.*

She sets to work.

Blackout.)